the skyline of information processing

edited by
h. zemanek

IFIP

north-holland

THE SKYLINE OF INFORMATION PROCESSING

Proceedings of the
Tenth Anniversary Celebration of the IFIP
Amsterdam, October 25, 1970

edited by
H. ZEMANEK
IFIP President 1971-74
IBM, Vienna, Austria

N·H
P C
1972

NORTH-HOLLAND PUBLISHING COMPANY – AMSTERDAM • LONDON

Library of Congress Catalog Card Number: 72–93499
ISBN North-Holland: 0 7204 2071 7

Published by
NORTH-HOLLAND PUBLISHING COMPANY – AMSTERDAM
NORTH-HOLLAND PUBLISHING COMPANY, LTD. – LONDON

PRINTED IN THE NETHERLANDS

CONTENTS

PREFACE

Time advances fast in Information Processing. IFIP, the International Federation for Information Processing, has already had its tenth anniversary – celebrated by a set of lectures in Amsterdam on the 25 October, 1970. A small Programme Committee, consisting of IFIP officers, selected the speakers – but the organization of the celebration was carried out by Professor A. van Wijngaarden, the representative of the IFIP member society from the Netherlands, the host of the event. It is a duty and a great pleasure for me to express here the thanks of IFIP for his efforts, which resulted in a most worthy and memorable day.

Fast advancing time hit the editor who had, as usual, to overcome a set of difficulties to get the book published – consequently with a certain delay. But the content of the lectures has in no way lost importance or actuality. It is to note with regret that one of the speakers did not submit his manuscript; the slot was filled by a contribution of another speaker to a later event which, however, not only fits perfectly but also completes the skyline. IFIP hopes that this small book will be useful for the information processing community and will show the spirit of IFIP.

The book is published by the North-Holland Publishing Co., Amsterdam: the traditional IFIP publisher. And it affords me further pleasure to mention IFIP's satisfaction with the excellent cooperation; more than a dozen IFIP publications document the activities – congresses, conferences and committee work – for the benefit of the community.

H. ZEMANEK
IFIP President 1971–74

INTRODUCTION TO THE MEETING

In 1959, ten years after the inauguration, in the United Kingdom, of the world's first stored-program computer, UNESCO sponsored the first International Conference on Information Processing. This Conference took place in Paris. In the planning meetings during the preceeding year, national representatives from nine countries met to organise the scientific program and to develop an international exhibition of information processing equipment. At the conference, almost 2000 delegates from 37 countries attended the scientific presentations.

Even before the conference, it was apparent that future international meetings and other activities were essential to the development of information sciences throughout the world and that the need existed for a suitable international body. Consequently, appropriate statuses were drafted, and IFIP came into existence, in January 1960, with thirteen national societies as members.

Since then, much has happened and it is a great honour for the Netherlands and the information processing professionalists in this country that the General Assembly has chosen the Netherlands as host country for a modest celebration of its tenth anniversary. We like IFIP, because on the one hand, our country has supported IFIP from the early beginning, contributing in the work of its Technical Committees, and Working Groups, as well as in the promotion of the IFIP Administrative Data Processing Group, whereas, on the other hand, IFIP has given our country the opportunity of worldwide, scientific contacts.

It is the strong hope and firm belief of the Netherlands information processing community that IFIP will expand its activities and will keep contributing towards a most efficient application of computers for the well being of men and society.

A. van WIJNGAARDEN

THE SPEAKERS
(in the order of presentation)

I. MALECKI
Director, Department of Science Policy and Promotion of Basic Sciences – United Nations Educational, Scientific and Cultural Organization (UNESCO), Paris (France).

G.B. GRESFORD
Director for Science and Technology – United Nations Organization (UN), New York (USA).

A.A. DORODNICYN
Academician, Director, Computing Center – Academy of Sciences, Moscow (USSR).
IFIP President 1968–1971, IFIP Trustee 1966–1968.

I.L. AUERBACH
President, Auerbach Corporation, Philadelphia (USA).
IFIP HONORARY MEMBER
IFIP President 1960–1965, IFIP Trustee 1966–1968.

A.P. SPEISER
Professor, ETH Zurich – Director of Research, Brown, Boveri & Cie, Baden (Switzerland).
IFIP President 1965–1968, IFIP Secretary 1960–1965.

D. CHEVION
Director, Office Mechanization Center – Ministry of Finance, Jerusalem (Israel).
IFIP Vice-President 1968–1971, IFIP Trustee 1965–1967.

F.L. BAUER
Professor, University of Technology, Munich (Germany).

A. van WIJNGAARDEN
Professor, Director, Mathematisch Centrum, Amsterdam (The Netherlands).
IFIP Vice-President 1962–1964, IFIP Trustee 1967–1970

H. ZEMANEK
Professor, University of Technology Vienna – Director, IBM Laboratory Vienna (Austria).
IFIP Vice-President 1968–1971, IFIP President 1971–1974.

H.B.G. CASIMIR
Vice-President, Royal Academy of Sciences, The Hague (The Netherlands).

OPENING ADDRESS

by

I. MALECKI
UNESCO, Paris

Upon reading the invitation to this celebration, one may ask why to celebrate such a short period of existence as ten years and why has Unesco been interested from the beginning in IFIP activity and, consequently, why have I, as the representative of this Organization, the honour to be invited to assist in one of the opening addresses?

I would like to reply to both questions of my imaginary interlocutor. In the XIXth century, the discovery of electricity increased a hundredfold the power of man, giving him a chance to free himself from psysical effort. The revolution of informatics, of which we are witness, is starting to increase a thousand times and, in several cases even a billion times, the speed and capacity of our thinking. The computer amplifies, but does not generate the ability to think. Its development does not liberate us from mental effort: on the contrary, the new possibility of computerizing can only blow up our own idea, showing its beauty or caricatural ugliness. At the same time, data storage and processing give quite new possibilities of worldwide dissemination of information, opening, even for use farest and poorest countries, the accessibility to the treasury of human knowledge.

That is why Unesco, having in its constitutions as one of its main goals to "develop and to increase the means of communication between the people and to employ these means for the purpose of mutual understanding ... by insisting methods of international co-operation calculated to give the people of all countries access to the printed and published materials produced by any of them" is so deeply interested in the national development of information processing which is one of the main elements of informatics development for the benefit of mankind.

During the last twenty years, three generations of computers have been set up. In comparison with three human generations of 30 years each, the relative age of the IFIP Organisation can be evaluated as at least 50 years. In the light of this approach, IFIP is not only an important but also a rather old distinguished organization and the celebration of this jubelee is fully justified.

May I on behalf of the Director-General of Unesco wish you during the next ten years the achievements compatible with another half a century of work spent in the improvement of new means of data processing.

Finally, I would like to express to you the profound hope of my Organisation that in the future the more and more powerful tool you are developing should be used to hasten the progress of human society, peace and creation and not to urge the war and destruction facilities.

OPENING ADDRESS

by

G. B. GRESFORD
United Nations, New York

It is an honour for me to be with you today to join in the 10th Anniversary Celebrations of the International Federation for Information Processing. In its short period of existence, IFIP has developed into a prestigeous instrument for international exchange and co-operation. This is of great significance since information processing is one of the most rapidly expanding fields in both developed and the developing countries, responding not only to the needs thrown up by the increasing complexity of development but also to the opportunities provided by progress in the relevant technologies.

In response to a resolution adopted at the 23rd session of the General Assembly in 1968, the Secretary-General of the United Nations has recently issued a report entitled "The Application of Computer Technology for Development" (document E/4800). I should like to take this opportunity to express our gratitude and appreciation to the International Federation for Information Processing for the assistance that it provided to the United Nations in the preparation of this report. The establishment by IFIP of its Special Committee for International Liaison for Governmental Organizations, under the chairmanship of Mr. Auerbach, has greatly facilitated the co-operation between IFIP and the UN in this matter.

The concern of United Nations for accelerating the development of the developing countries is more marked than ever in this year in which the 25th Anniversary of the United Nations is being celebrated. Much has been said about the need to find ways of drawing more effectively upon modern technology for accelerating the rate of economic and social progress of the developing countries. The economically-sound and practical application of computer technology in the developing countries can contribute considerably to this end, and will require, *inter alia*, the strong interest and involvement of the international professional community drawn both from developed and the developing countries and from countries having differing economic and political systems. IFIP has a continuing critical role to play in contributing to this objective in the years ahead.

In the Secretary-General's report (document E/4800), the principal recommendations and conclusions draw attention to the role of education and training for computer technology in the developing countries, to computer facilities and services, and to the strategies and policies that developing countries need to formulate and follow in applying computer technology in the context of their development.

On the institutional side, one recommendation in the report calls for consideration of a proposal to establish, under the principal organs of the United Nations, an international advisory board on the application of computer technology for development. The two broad types of function that might be envisaged for such board are:

(a) To promote the application of computer technology for development through international co-operative efforts in association with the United Nations family of organizations;

(b) To provide, upon request, independent and objective advice to assist developing countries in their decisions on the use of computer technology for their development.

It is further envisaged that there might be representatives on the board of the major international professional organizations such as IFIP.

It will be recognized that although the proposed new board would not be regarded as an illusion for real activity, such an organizational arrangement would permit a focal point to be created that would give continuing attention as to how computer technology might be applied on a sound basis to assist the progress of the developing countries. The participation of the international professional organizations such as IFIP on this board would represent an important innovation in structure, and could assist in ensuring a more balanced view of the part that computer technology can play in the processes of development. The involvement of the professional community through bodies such as IFIP in international co-operative activities can provide complimentarity to the efforts of governments and of inter-governmental institutions.

In this year in which there are the 10th Anniversary Celebrations of IFIP and the 25th Anniversary of the United Nations, it seems appropriate to seek effective ways whereby common aspirations of both bodies may be furthered. The knowledge, experience and interest of IFIP can contribute to the realization of the expectations of many of the developing countries and can reflect the co-operation of its members drawn from as many countries as possible. In the 1970s, in the Second United Nations Development Decade, we believe that the developing countries will need to call more fully on relevant technology to accelerate their development; computer technology, as all here will agree, is one important element in determining the rate of technological change. As was mentioned in the Secretary-General's report, "the continuing growth of computer technology and its application in the industrialized countries will be a general feature of the

1970s. Increasingly, it is being recognized that in itself the computer is not a panacea and that all the difficulties and consequences of using computer technology need to be considered". Finally, it needs emphasis that a long-term commitment will be required by the individual governments of developing countries, and this in turn may contribute to lessening the gap between the developed and the developing countries in the application of computer technology.

TEN YEARS OF IFIP

by

A. A. DORODNICYN

Moscow

The idea of organizing an international federation on information processing first appeared in 1959, when an initiative group of representatives from different countries gathered together, during the first International Congress on Information Processing in Paris, to discuss the problems of international cooperation in that field. They came to the conclusion that the creation of an international federation was necessary, and in 1960 the Federation on Information Processing was formally organised and received the now well-known name "IFIP". And that is why we celebrate today the tenth anniversary of IFIP.

The question can be put: was it not too late for organizing such a federation?

Really, in 1959, fifteen years had passed since the first electronic digital computer was constructed; at that time industrial production of the second generation computers had already begun.

But the understanding of the importance of computers did not come at once. Just at that time the wide circles of scientists and engineers began to realise the fact that computers are not merely fast arithmometers but something much more essential, I would say – the intellectual helpers of man. And just this property of computers opens such huge fields for their application, that even now it is impossible to foresee to what changes they will bring the human society.

If we throw a retrospective look on the development of computer science during the past decade, it is difficult indeed not to be surprised by the speed with which this science penetrated in the life of mankind. I emphasize: in the life of mankind, not only in separate domains of science or technology.

Scientists of different specialities – beginning with physicists and finishing with sociologists – use computers in their research; managers of undertakings, presidents of companies are already unable to act without the help of computers; political leaders use computers for analysing political situations. It is likely that soon even house cooks will be unable to prepare lunch without terminals in their kitchens.

The tempo with which the industry of computers increases surpasses the tempo of development in any other branch of industry. Education of specialists in information processing (hardware, software, application) has in many countries taken the first place in respect to their number.

Such an exceptional position in computer science, as a science penetrating to all fields of human activity, set IFIP, at the front line of this expansion, a difficult task.

And we tried to do our best, but of course it is your prerogative to judge about our successes.

We had to find new, effective forms in international cooperation. In the majority of international scientific unions the main form of cooperation is organization of congresses, conferences etc. Despite the importance of all these forms IFIP could not limit its activity to them.

And perhaps the main part of the IFIP activity goes through Special Interest Group (SIG), Technical Committees and Working Groups, which often work out quite concrete problems of general importance. As results of such activities Terminological Dictionary, Subset ALGOL, ALGOL 68 can be mentioned.

Just these forms alone give a permanent character to co-operation in IFIP and induce and help to establish cooperation between institutions in different countries and between different people.

Computer Science is very suitable for international co-operation. To explain what I mean, let us compare our field with, say, atomic physics or space exploration. Any considerable contribution in those two last fields can be made by practically rich countries only, because they need very large financial and material expenses. But success in computer science (especially in application) depends mainly on good human brains and talented people.

All my life experience has persuaded me that all people, all nations, all races are equally wise, equally talented and therefore, an important contribution in computer science with the same probability can be made by a man from a rich country as well as from a poor one.

And it is a pleasure for me to announce that just here in Amsterdam all the continents became represented in IFIP.

The celebration of an anniversary has sense only on condition that it compels the heroes of festivity to think through to their future, and it is especially important in the case of a subject developing as rapidly as information processing.

This fast development makes it very difficult to forecast the achievements in our field and I'll not try to do this. But what does seem possible is to foresee the main directions in which computer science will proceed.

I see here three main flows:

1. Development of large computer systems for collective use.
2. Elaboration of scientific methods for "Governing of Society".
3. Working out exact, algorithmical methods of investigation in descriptive (non-mathematical) sciences.

It is now clear to everybody that systems for collective use are the most rational in the use of computers. And not only because it is the cheapest way for users, but – what is much more important – only in the powerful computing or information centers can all necessary information for users be accumulated. When interconnected systems of computer centers come into existence, then in principle all the information accumulated by human society can be stored in such systems.

A very remarkable phenomenon of our time is the increase in the number of computer users. People very far from mathematics or computer science become computer users. No doubt this process will develop rapidly. People want to use computers as they use telephones – having no knowledge as to how automatic telephone centers are constructed or how they work. Only a minimum set of rules is necessary for telephone use and people need a similar approach to computer use. In developing the systems for collective use this demand of society has to be taken into account.

Of course, the creation of large computer systems is a very great problem. It contains hardware, logical structure, software, languages and many other technical, logical and organizational (including educational) problems.

Governing of society – this is the final aim of the problem. And the problem consists in removing contradictions between the *aims* of this governing and the *methods* for achieving them. Remember how often we see striking contradictions between declarations by political leaders of their aims and their real deeds, real results.

The *man in the street* usually explains this phenomenon by the assumption that all politicians are dishonest men. I don't think it is the general case. I believe that more often politicians do indeed want to achieve their declared aims, but they can't find the way to do this. Intuition helps a man in relatively simple cases, but is of no use in complicated situations. Governing of society is perhaps the most complicated, the most manifold problem, including economical, social, psychological and political questions.

Only a scientific approach to the problem, the elaboration

of quantative and logical methods in analysis of situations and results of decisions, can help to avoid the contradictions mentioned.

As I said, the governing of society is the final aim. Many steps must be done for approaching it. Administrative and economical data processing in their contemporary state are the first steps in this direction. Optimal planning is perhaps the second. But all this is the beginning of starting the construction of a bridge between aims and means.

Underlining the problem of introducing exact methods to descriptive sciences I don't want to diminish the importance of mathematical methods in traditionally exact sciences. Just the surprisingly swift successes in mechanics and physics in the last twenty-five years would have been impossible without wide use of computers. But here the problem consists in perfection of methods, not invention of quite new approaches.

All exact sciences, except perhaps mathematics, were formerly descriptive. Their history convincingly shows that fast successes in the sciences of biological and humanitary cycles are impossible without elaboration of appropriate mathematical methods (understanding under this expression exactly formulated algorithms, though not necessarily computational). And these successes are sharply demanded by the population of our overcrowded planet.

Demands always rouse the corresponding actions and more attempts are always made for application of mathematical methods in the sciences of the cycles mentioned. Some of them are quite successful, but we have to be careful and know to distinguish the real results from idle talking.

It is interesting to note that as a rule successes are obtained by mathematicians but not by specialists of that concrete science. Mathematicians like to explain this by the assumption that they are wiser than other people. That is, of course, unjustified ambition. The real cause lays in the education of thinking. To illustrate the idea I relate the following case.

Once three people – a sociologist, a physicist and a mathematician were walking somewhere in the country. Suddenly they saw a herd of cows. "*All* the cows are black" – exclaimed the sociologist. The physicist corrected him: "All the cows *in this herd* are black". The mathematician looked and said – "All the cows in this herd, *seen from this side*, are black."

That is a pretty good example of an exact description of facts, and just the mixture of facts and conjectures is the first difficulty which a mathematician meets trying to understand the content of some descriptive science as a term or sometimes even as a fundamental notion, but having no definition (from the mathematician's point of view).

It seems that separation of facts and formalisation of notions is the most elaborate part of the work in the solution of the problem, though only a preliminary one.

Thus the future activity of IFIP has to meet the trends in computer science, and as you see it is in no way an easy task. For, to fulfil it IFIP needs men of different specialities, different tastes and styles, who want to work for his organization.

At last the men determine the success of the work. The past decade was not bad for IFIP and for all our achievements we have to thank the men of our federation. It is, therefore, a great pleasure and honour for me to express IFIP's recognition of the merits of our distinguished members, who have made a very essential contribution for the prosperity of IFIP.

This recognition is symbolically represented by small souvenirs which IFIP presents to them. Let me give the names of these distinguished men:

Mr. I. Auerbach – the first President and now Honorary Member of IFIP.

Prof. A. Speiser – the second President of IFIP and Secretary-Treasurer for the first 6 years.

Prof. A. van Wijngaarden – the first Vice-President of IFIP and organizer of this anniversary conference.

Prof. L. Łukasiewicz – the second Vice-President of IFIP.
Mr. Carteron – the former Secretary-Treasurer of IFIP, our Chairman of Statutes and By-Laws Committee now.

I hope they will continue their remarkable work for IFIP in the future.

I.L. AUERBACH, IFIP HONORARY MEMBER

The few words of President Dorodnicyn which were an introduction to the ceremony of handing over the presents mentioned, were followed by the official announcement of I.L. Auerbach, the initiator and first President of IFIP, as an Honorary Member.

Isaac L. Auerbach, born 1921, graduated 1943 from Drexel Institute of Technology (B.S.), and 1947 from Harvard University (M.S.). He joined Remington Rand, then became director of special products with Burroughs. End 1957 he formed his own company. He pioneered development and use of magnetic cores in digital communications and in computer memories.

He is a Fellow of IEEE since 1958 and of AAAS since 1969.

As mentioned by Mr. Malecki, UNESCO responded to the initiative of a group of people under the leadership of I.L. Auerbach when they sponsored and housed the ICIP 1959, and it was essentially this same group which brought IFIP into existence. I.L. Auerbach was elected President in 1960 and reelected in 1963; during his term the technical committees 1 through 4 were started; he was responsible for the Congresses 1962 in Munich and 1965 in New York and his valuable advice has been available for everybody in IFIP since then. His election as an Honorary Member is only a minor acknowledgment of his services to IFIP.

NEED FOR AN INFORMATION SYSTEMS THEORY

by

I. L. AUERBACH
Philadelphia

The problem and the need

The field of information processing is on the horns of a dilemma. Rapid advances in computing hardware have outdistanced any development in the methodology, technology, and theory of information systems.

The speed with which the electronic digital computer, invented in 1945, was adopted by nearly every segment of our society has been unmatched in the history of technology. In 25 short years the computer has spawned the third largest industry in the world. It has become a commonplace office and business commodity. Its use is being taught to elementary school children. No other invention of man has proliferated so swiftly or had so profound an impact on our daily lives in such a short time.

There is no need to mention to this audience the uniqueness of the computer in comparison with all other machines invented to date. Almost all other machines were invented to do something when switched on. Unless a computer has been instructed what to do through its program, the only thing it does when switched on is make a little heat and very little light. The computer is unique as an invention in that it requires a detailed program to govern its operation.

The design of computer hardware and software to produce an effective information processing system is more an *art* than a science. No absolute means exist to measure the efficiency or effectiveness of an information system. There are few, if any, scientific theories for predicting what will happen in an information system under various conditions.

The failure of information systems design methodology to keep pace with the capabilities of computers and the demands of its users has caused a problem of crisis proportion for the information processing industry. Information systems are difficult to specify adequately by their users, and they do not have a suitable specification language which deals with information flow and end use. It is difficult to speak about information as *information* without reducing it to *data processing* terms and as a result, we often impose an inelegant or restrictive solution in the very way we pose the problem.

Correlated with the problem of specification, yet manifesting itself as a separate problem, we find that information systems cannot be designed, built and evaluated with adequate effectiveness. Too frequently too many designers approach too many problems as exercises requiring original creativity. The predictable result is that the system built is unique and is

- not adaptable to different problem environments
- not easily maintained, and
- not economic.

Analysis

These problems are symptomatic of the lack of an adequate basis in the methodology, technology, and theory of information systems and/or a lack of disciplined application of the methodology and technology we do possess. We are cursed with the problem of the large, complex system – problems of dimensionality and scale – for which there is neither an adequate science nor an adequate engineering discipline.

The problem has been compounded by laying too much stress on what poses for efficiency as a design criterion; namely, speed of computation, in terms of the number of machine instructions executed. This is well understood, we can measure it, and it has become the accepted measure of computational efficiency.

Unfortunately, in information systems this type of efficiency is often bought at too high a price: namely, lack of structural modularity. More stress should be placed on structural modularity and the utilization of predeveloped, pretested, multipurpose elements, as well as tolerance to abnormal traffic and error conditions as measures of system effectiveness.

Too often trial and error is the practiced methodology to match an information processing system to the need. The heuristic approach is still the rule rather than the exception in a computer systems design.

From an information systems designer's point of view, there remains the inability to specify the characteristics of the system in advance so that it is possible to devise a test which can serve as an acceptance criterion. That is, we lack the ability to establish evaluation criteria with sufficient specificity to enable a third party to decide whether or not the specifications and the users needs have been fulfilled. Certainly, this facet is one of the major shortcomings in the evolution of the field of programming.

An example from another field akin to our own will illustrate this point. One will admit that it is possible today to specify the characteristics of an electric power generation station and transmission lines to provide electrical energy to a small town so that manufacturing companies from all parts of the world can respond to this need in sufficient detail to permit evaluation of proposals and be certain that the selected and delivered equipment will meet the specifications.

We lack a comparable capacity in the information systems field. Instead, the *component parts* of the system are specified with the hope that the resulting composite system will perform the functions required.

In defining the information systems requirements, frequently the real problem is not clearly known or, even worse, is incorrectly defined. As a result good solutions are formulated to wrong problems. System specifications may propagate incorrect problem definitions that are biased by the designer's experience so that they will reflect the limitations and errors of other systems. Empirical solutions are frequently "force-fits" and inefficient solutions to the problem.

Economically, the entire computer field is in trouble. A recent survey concluded that in the commercial field, from a profit standpoint, computer efforts in all but a few exceptional companies are in real, often unacknowledged trouble.

Faster – costlier – more sophisticated hardware; more involved and complex programs; larger and increasingly costly computer staffs; increasingly complex and ingenious applications are in evidence everywhere. Less and less in evidence as these new applications proliferate are successful and/or profitable results!

The scarcity of *qualified* people to design and program these systems is severe. The exceedingly high cost of programming itself is rapidly approaching the economic breakpoint. The difficulty to adequately train qualified university graduates to become competent professionals in our field is already well known.

We are like the Romans in the application of inventions to the solution of problems. What the information systems field needs is something akin to the Age of Pericles in Greece. That was the day of Plato, Archimedes, and Euclid: a time when the realization first dawned that physical phenomena could be comprehended as mental abstractions.

For all of our progress, we lack a firm intellectual base. We have few axioms, postulates or theorems or laws. We are in need of some basic rules such as Boyle's law for understanding gases or Coulomb's law on the forces exerted between electrical charges or the Carnot cycle for defining the ideal performance for a heat engine.

Speaking as basically a pragmatic and impatient technocrat trained in engineering and physics and deeply concerned about the economics of our industry, I assert that we badly – very badly – need a scientific base for the information processing industry.

Solution

Let me offer one very important step – the industry will not pass through the crisis until it has learned that an information *process* is not the same thing as an information *system* and has learned how to specify each.

An information *process* is something that is active and when we describe it, we are describing *behavior*. We need descriptive languages for information and the transformations on information that do not require that we also specify the how and the means.

On the other hand, it should be possible to describe information *systems* as *structures* which operate on *data divorced from information content.* Here we require structure-describing languages, and our operations are those of building and transforming structures and operators rather than information.

The pertinent evaluation criteria from a process or behavioral point of view are quite different from evaluation criteria approached from a structural point of view.

The pertinent questions from an information *process* point of view have to do with information structures, data streams, and user actions and reactions.

The pertinent questions from a *systems* point of view have to do with the architecture of the system, its modules, and their interfaces.

When we have standards and specification languages for information *processes* we will be able to specify information processing problem requirements and information structures without implying a solution or system structure *and* we will be able to specify tests or measurements which assure acceptable processing results.

When we have standards and specification languages for information *systems* we will be able to create system structures which reduce to a minimum those structural elements which must be unique for this instance of the problem. That is, we will be able to specify and measure *structural* efficiency.

Progress towards an information systems design discipline

However basic the need for theory, the information processing industry will benefit first from advances in methodology and technology, rather than the theoretical aspects of information systems science. There are some small signs that progress is being made.

In the area of modular systems, systems whose overall structure permits routine substitution and/or augmentation of operational modules with standardized interfaces, we see some success with systems oriented for scientific computation in which the *data structures* are vectors and matrices, but only faint progress with systems which handle the complex data structures needed for business information processing.

A good example of a system whose overall architecture and control philosophy leads to the complete modularity of operators and data known as "coherent" systems is the online computational system at MIT's Lincoln Laboratory called Reckoner/Mediator, designed by Harris & Hill, senior scientists of my company.

There has been recent evidence that generalized data management systems will soon be able to provide a much needed additional level of software structure between the computer and the data processing application.

This will allow the systems designer to utilize a generalized module for many data management functions in an information system, the definition, storage, retrieval, and transformation of a broad class of data structures.

We have been working on this problem at AUERBACH for many years and some useful progress has been made.

Generalized data management systems such as these permit libraries or operational modules (tasks or jobs) accessible to the executive control system, to be created. These modules can then be invoked (executed) upon use of the command, that is the name of the module, in the job control language.

The standardization of languages for describing data and procedures will play an important role in insuring the transportability of data and programs from one environment to another.

Considerable progress has been made in the area of *procedural* languages – I think the work being done on ALGOL 68 represents a major step forward – however, efforts at developing *data description* languages are just starting to get underway in groups such as CODASYL's systems committee and SICFIDET, ACM's special interest committee on file definition and translation.

What is required here is a comprehensive system of data describing languages suitable for the many levels at which data is transported and manipulated, from the cell structures suitable for mapping onto addressable storage to the completely device-independent information item structures of interest to management-level users.

We in the information processing industry are well aware of the difficulties of managing a large information system development project. Recent studies (Ref: SDC [28]) have shown that there has been a variance of an order-of-magnitude in the per-instruction development costs of large real-time information processing systems of comparable size.

This is symptomatic of the fact that the information processing industry has not been disciplined in the application of sound program management methods. The U.S. government, who has paid for the development of many of these systems, has recently developed a set of standards, called Configuration Management Standards (Ref: Ratynski, et al. [26]) for the control of large hardware/software system projects, including documentation and testing standards.

These standards promise to impose on software development projects the same management disciplines which are now taken for granted in hardware development. We also see emerging the application of computers to the problem of project management, not only for rapid accounting of project expenditures, but for optimum scheduling of project manpower and effort, and monitoring of progress.

There has been a growing interest in the development of a theory for large systems. One line of development has been general systems theory, the application of mathematical methods, especially graph theory, relation theory, and matrix theory, to the analysis of large multi-variable systems. The emphasis has been on general tools applicable to the analysis of systems, biological as well as mechanical (Ref: Bertalanffy [34]; Wymore [36]; Zadeh [38]).

Very little work has been specifically directed to large man/machine information systems.

In addition to this work in general systems theory there has been some progress made in the theory of computational structures and computational schemata (Ref: Luconi [20], Dennis [10], Holt [18]).

Here we see the beginnings of a theory which has the potential of providing tools useful at the engineering level for representing information systems, especially predicting and resolving conflicts arising from the interaction of independently defined but simultaneously operating, subprocesses.

Summary

We still desperately need a workable, comprehensive, theoretical foundation for information processing. The key to this theory appears to be the application of the appropriate mathematical tools, especially graph and relation theory, and the formalization of appropriate languages for the information systems designer.

Languages are needed to serve as tools in three distinct areas:

(a) the communication of user problems in terms of information structures and their transformation,

(b) the description of the *behavior* of information systems, and,

(c) the description of the *structure* of information systems.

It appears that only the second of these is served by procedural languages, and only in the current ALGOL 68 activity do we see an effort directed to the development of a language with the appropriate scope and rigor. This does not imply that I feel that ALGOL 68, per se, is the last word in procedural languages, or is actually adequate for that purpose. It is just that ALGOL 68 seems to have attacked the problem with the required breadth of scope, including linguistic rigor, with formal specification of syntax and semantics, and a wide range of data and program structures.

However, we require much more emphasis on non-procedural languages for representing computational schemata.

The other two areas:

– languages for describing *information* structures, and

– languages for describing *system* structures

have received much less emphasis from the computing field and therefore are far less developed.

We should see a correspondingly greater emphasis in these areas in the future.

Before we can call our field a science, there must be:

– a distinguishable body of knowledge
– general concepts, principles and analytical expressions that explain cause and effect
– a rigorous definition of the fundamental quantities involved, and
– a means for quantification.

These ideas must be amenable to scientific method, that is, the repeatability of experiments yielding the same results and scientific theories for information processing that allow exploration of not only what happens in an information system but why it happens and, more importantly, to predict what will happen if certain conditions are changed. It is not to be assumed that these are the only elements needed to call the field a science but they are certainly a good start.

A theory is an attempt to provide a logical, clear, and well-rounded explanation of an event or group of events. A scientist first collects and studies all the available information relating to a given topic; then he attempts to fit these facts together in some definite, orderly pattern that will enable him to understand not merely *what* has happened, but *how* and *why* it has happened.

A sound theory has two values: first, it offers a reasonable explanation for a set of known facts; second, it enables the scientist to predict, and thus makes possible an extension of the field of man's knowledge.

For example, Maxwell's theory of electricity in the nineteenth century predicted the existence of radio waves long before they were actually produced by Hertz. If, as time goes on, additional facts are discovered that cannot be satisfactorily explained by an accepted theory, this theory must be either completely discarded, or else modified in such a way that it does explain the new information. This process of improving accepted scientific theories is going on all the time.

Finally, it is clear that the field of information sciences is in a transitional mode and very much in need of new and creative thinking that will evolve a set of axioms, postulates, laws and theorems that will explain the information system. These might best be set forth in the following list:

- a body of theoretical and methodological knowledge
- general principles applicable to a variety of problems
- measures and criteria for quantifying variables
- tools, techniques and research methods for dealing with problems
- experiments which can be conducted with rigor with the results reproducible
- existence of a group of people with a common interest and jargon who are working on problems of a similar nature
- special educational preparation to enter the field
- an underlying philosophy that can yield an ideal system
- valid formulae that lead to numerical values
- precise and rigorous definitions of the elements involved (e.g., information, data, etc.) their states, quantities, composition, properties and behavior.

I hope that these thoughts have identified the need for and fruitful avenues of research to create an information systems theory.

Bibliography

[1] I.L. Auerbach, Information Science – The Broader View. (In L. Schultz, ed. Sixth Annual National Colloquium on Information Retrieval, Philadelphia, Medical Documentation Service, 1969, p. 1–7.)

[2] I.L. Auerbach, Technological Forecast 1970. Paper presented before the UCLA "Symposium on Expanding Use of Computers in the 70's", University of California, Los Angeles, March 30, 1970.

[3] Y. Bar-Hillel and R. Carnap, Semantic Information, in: Jackson, Willis, eds. *Communication Theory* (Butterworths, London, 1953) p. 503–13.

[4] J. Belzer, Education in Information Science, Journal of the American Society for Information Science 21 (4): 269–73, July-August 1970.

[5] H. Borko, Information Science: What Is It?, American Documentation 19(1): 3–5, Jan. 1968.
[6] L. Brillouin, *Science and Information Theory,* 2d ed. (Academic Press, New York, 1964).
[7] L. Brillouin, *Scientific Uncertainty and Information* (Academic Press, New York, 1964).
[8] R. Carnap and Y. Bar-Hillel, An Outline of a Theory of Semantic Information, MIT Research Lab. Electronics, Tech. Report. 247. 1953.
[9] C. Cherry, *On Human Communication* (MIT Press, Cambridge, Mass. 1966).
[10] J.B. Dennis, *Computational Structures.* MIT (Course Notes, See Chapter 7 Computational Schemata).
[11] A. Fairthorne, The Scope and Aims of the Information Sciences and Technologies (Preprint prepared for presentation at the International Congress of Scientific Information, Moscow, September 1968).
[12] S. Gorn, The Computer and Information Sciences: A New Basic Discipline, SIAM Review 5(2): 150–5, April 1963.
[13] S. Gorn, The Individual and Political Life of Information Systems, in: Heilprin, L.B. et al, (eds.) Proceedings of the Symposium on Education for Information Science, (Spartan, Washington, 1965) p. 33–40.
[14] W.P. Harris and P.B. Hill, The Reckoner and the Mediator: A consumer oriented on-line system, in: A.J.H. Morrell (ed.), Information Processing 68 (North-Holland, Amsterdam, 1969).
[15] R.V.L. Hartley, Transmission of Information, Bell System Technical Journal, 7:535–63, July 1928 (monograph 343).
[16] J.F. Harvey, Professional Aspects of Information Science and Technology, in: C.A. Guadra, (ed.) *Annual Review of Information Science and Technology,* Vol. 2 (Interscience, New York, 1967) p. 419–42.
[17] C.F. Hockett, An Approach to the Quantification of Semantic Noise, Philosophical Science 19: 257–60, 1952.
[18] A.W. Holt, Information System Theory Project, RADC-TR-68-306 (Sept. 1968) (AD 676972).
[19] Liebowitz: The Technical Specification – Key to Management Control of Computer Programming. SJCC 67. p. 51–60.
[20] F.L. Luconi, Output Functional Computer Structures. MIT, Project MAC.
[21] C.J. Maloney, Semantic Information, American Documentation 13:276–286, 1962.
[22] A.R. Meetham, Communication Theory and the Evaluation of Information Retrieval Systems, Information Storage and Retrieval 5:129–34, 1969.
[23] K. Otten and A. Debons, Towards a Metascience of Information: Informatology, Journal of the American Society for Information Science 21(1): 89–94, Jan/Feb 1970.
[24] B. Payne, A Descriptive Theory of Information, Behavioral Science 11(4): 295–305, 1966.
[25] A.D. Pratt, An Essay on the Nature of Information, American Documentation Institute, Proceedings Vol. 4: 3–7, Oct. 1967.
[26] M.V. Ratynski, The Air Force Computer Program Acquisition Concept, SJCC 67. p. 33–44.

[27] C. Reno, Computers are for Concepts, Journal of the American Society for Information Science, 21 (4): 298–98, July-Aug. 1970.
[28] SDC (no author): Development of Equations for Estimating the Cost of Computer Programs. SDC, June 1966. (AD 637 760).
[29] L.V. Searle and G. Neil, Configuration Management of Computer Programs by the Air Force: Principles and Documentation, SJCC 67. p. 45–50.
[30] C.E. Shannon and W. Weaver, *The Mathematical Theory of Communication,* (University of Illinois Press, Urbana, Ill. 1949).
[31] Yu. A. Shreider, On the Quantitative Characteristics of Semantic Information, Nauch.-Tekh. Inform. (10): 33–38, 1963 (in Russian).
[32] D.L. Szekely, On Firmer Intellectual Bases for Computer Science, Computerworld 4 (35): 12, Sept. 2, 1970.
[33] R.S. Taylor, Professional Aspects of Information Science and Technology, in: C.A. Cuadra, ed., *Annual Review of Information Science and Technology,* Vol. 1 (Interscience, New York, 1966) p. 15–40.
[34] L. von Bertalanffy, An Outline of General System Theory, British J. Philos. Science 1 (1950) 139.
[35] H.M. Weisman, Information and the Discipline of Communication Sciences, American Documentation Institute, Proceedings.
[36] A.W. Wymore, *A Mathematical Theory of Systems Engineering – The Elements.* (Wiley, New York, 1967).
[37] M.C. Yovits, Information Science: Toward the Development of a True Scientific Discipline, American Documentation 20 (5): 369–76, Oct. 1969.
[38] L.A. Zadeh and C.A. Desoer, *Linear System Theory* (McGraw-Hill, 1963).

COMPUTERS AND TECHNOLOGY

by

A. P. SPEISER
Baden

Justification

At first glance it might seem like a strange undertaking to attempt to talk about the relations between computers and technology. Are not computers technological devices? Are they not often taken to represent technological progress per se? In the broader sense this is of course true; but among all products of technology computers occupy a very special place. They are the tools of what is often called the second industrial revolution; they progress at an almost incredibly rapid rate; and, what is perhaps most important, they possess the unique dichotomy of hardware and software. It is therefore a special challenge to meditate for half an hour on the relations between technology and one of its own implementations.

The impact of technology on computers

It is sometimes said that among all the major technical innovations computers are the most important and have the most far-reaching effects. Probably it is still too early to confirm this; as yet, electricity and television have a much more profound effect on our lives than computers. One observation, however, can be made: Among the major technical innovations, computers are the one which have gone the way from laboratory models to full maturity and worldwide penetration within the shortest time by far. The first electronic high-speed computer was operative in 1945 in the USA; the first stored-program computers – they were strictly laboratory versions – were tested in 1949 in Britain. By 1956, computers were produced by the thousands, and tape drives and disc memories were available. No doubt this can be considered as a certain level of maturity, even though these machines were largely based on tubes, not transistors. The time from first model to maturity therefore lasted between 7 and 11 years, depending on where we place the start. Compare this with the other technical innovations that we consider important such as the telephone, the electric light, the automobile, radio and television! With them, it is more difficult to determine the dates of start as well as the points in time of where maturity was reached, but there is not the slightest doubt that the growing-up period was longer by a factor of 3 or even more. It is this contrast which has led many people to conclude that today the process of technological innovation, in other words the path from a scientific discovery to a mature product, has become much faster and shorter. I thoroughly disagree with the conclusion in this generality, and I could cite many counter-examples, among which nuclear energy is the most striking. Rather, I consider computers to be an exceptional case, a case which is not likely to repeat even a few times in a century. It is worthwhile to dwell for a moment on the reasons for this anomaly.

Computers are based on the concept of the stored program, an idea conceived by one of the brilliant minds of our time, John von Neumann. Revolutionary ideas of this type normally require for their implementation lengthy and tedious technical developments. Take the automobile as an example: Before automobiles could be used on a large scale, such seemingly unrelated problems as the refining of oil and the improvement of rubber tires had to be solved. Computers, in contrast, were fortunate in that they could be rested on four cornerstones, represented by four technologies which had been developed for other purposes, in different parts of the world, and which were ready for use by anyone who cared to help himself:

– Pulse circuits
– Ferrites
– Magnetic recording
– Transistors.

Let me examine these fields briefly. Before the war, *pulse circuits* were a curiosity of the physical laboratory. Under the pressure of World War II, they were developed into an established technique with design rules based on sound physical principles, mostly at the Radiation Laboratory of M.I.T. and at the Royal Radar Establishment. These design rules could be adopted to digital circuits almost without change. *Ferrites* constitute a discovery which is based on a deep understanding of the quantum mechanics of ferro-magnetism, made in Holland; these materials were immediately grabbed by computer people when they needed core memories. *Magnetic recording* was brought to maturity by the need to record broadcast programs and for home entertainment; its principles were quickly adapted to magnetic drum memories, tape units and disc stores. Finally, *transistors* were an offspring of Radar work and were the result of a deep physical insight into the behaviour of semiconducting materials.

These four technologies, as I said, were ready to be used by anyone who cared to do so, and computer people were fast at grabbing what was available. It is good to note that none of these four technologies had been developed with computers in mind; the motive was a different one in each case. All had made their main steps forward between 1940 and 1950. Thus, when they were needed, they could be adopted to computers almost without change. This wonderful coincidence, which rarely occurs in history, in my opinion is responsible for the almost unbelievably fast progress of computers.

You will note that I have listed transistors as one of the four cornerstones. Actually, this item is somewhat different from the other three: They were not yet ready for the first computer pioneers. Before 1954 nobody seriously attempted to build a transistorised computer for commercial production. Thus we were forced – figuratively speaking – to make a big detour and to adapt vacuum tubes to a task for which they were really quite unsuited. The fact that machines with thousands of tubes operated reliably under field conditions is a great tribute to the engineers who developed them. It is interesting to speculate what would have happened if the computer age would have started 5 years later, or if transistors had been available 5 years earlier: A large and expensive effort would have been avoided.

As we may see from the foregoing, the relations between computers and technology in the early years have been unusual and most interesting. How about the subsequent years, the present, and the future? In the 1950's a number of discoveries and inventions were made which, as it was believed, would have a major impact on computers: Cryotrons, optical and even chemical devices, tunnel diodes, a large variety of magnetic devices, parametric amplifiers and, somewhat later, the injection laser. None of these expectations were fulfilled. The inventive technologist has to make an observation which to him must be very disappointing: Besides the four cornerstones which I have mentioned, only one item, the field effect transistor, has gained any degree of importance in computers. Moreover, it looks as if this statement would hold true for several more years to come. (The notion is of course used that integrated circuits, although they constitute a major step foreward, are not fundamentally different from transistors). The tremendous inventive and developmental effort which was spent on new devices has been in vain.

Nonetheless, computers have progressed at a very rapid rate. Most numerically defined parameters which characterise technology, such as computing speed and volumetric density, have increased at a rate of about 50% each year for the past 20 years. This rate of progress far exceeds most other fields of technology: It means a 10-fold increase in 6 years, 60-fold in 10 years. How long can this continue? Exponential trend-extrapolation is a pleasant game, but it is often overdone. Exponential trends cannot last for ever. I believe however it is safe to predict that, without radical changes, another factor of 10 can be obtained at the same rate of progress. This would carry us through 1976. As to an analysis of the more distant future, I suggest we gather again in 1980 for the IFIP 20-year-anniversary and see what the computer world looks like at that time!

The impact of computers on technology

In the previous chapter we have used some examples to study the impact which technological developments have had on the evolution of computers. It is worthwhile now to illuminate the converse process for a moment – the impact which computers are having on technological progress. The most obvious segment of course is the part of technology which may lead to improved computers. An early and impressive example are reliable vacuum tubes. In the early days it became quickly clear that computers could not be built with tubes that have an expected lifetime of 1000 hours or so. The ensuing pressure led to the development of much more reliable tubes, a result that heretofore had been declared impossible. Today computers are a multi-billion dollar business, and it is obvious that their needs must have a major impact on technical progress. For example, most of the advances in integrated circuits are stimulated by computer needs. Computer companies themselves operate large research laboratories, and the excellent scientific work they do has led to some fallout whose significance goes far beyond computers, such as the Gunn effect.

The impact of computers on technology however goes far beyond computer components and devices. It is clear that the ability of computers to perform large and complex calculations is now having a major impact on technical progress. Computers were originally conceived as time and labour saving devices, but they quickly evolved into machines that opened completely new possibilities. It is hardly necessary to enumerate many examples to this audience. We all know that modern airplanes would be impossible without computers. Steam turbines look very conservative to the outside observer; yet, today's largest units are vastly different from those of 10 years ago – not so much in principle, but in detail – and much of the progress is due to computer design methods.

Nuclear reactors are an interesting case in point: They constitute a new field of technology, a field which matured only after computers were available. As a consequence, design methods rely heavily on computers. The high cost of making experiments as well as the fact that catastrophic events must be avoided at all cost due to their disastrous effects have led to the practice of varying a design along almost every conceivable parameter by computation before implementing it. Without computers this would clearly be impossible. Accordingly, reactor development establishments are major computer users.

Computers and space

Space technology and space travel are among the most dramatic of today's technological achievements. No doubt, to the man on the street the result of landing a man on the moon is impressive and easily understandable – more easily than, say, the discovery of the laser principle. Still, many serious observers criticise the space program because of its magnitude. They say the large amounts of money should be used for more useful purposes. I disagree with them. The importance of the space programs should not be underestimated; there is no doubt in my mind that future historians – even those of the quite distant future – will regard the first landing of humans on the moon as an event of the very first order of importance, of an order that occurs only once within several centuries. It would be a mistake to regard this as a more or less useless expenditure of money.

To a technologically minded person, the space program is so impressive mainly because of its highly interdisciplinary aspect. (By "space program" I now mean the one about which most information is available, which is the U.S. Program). The very highest level of effort had to be mustered from fields such as celestial mechanics, structural engineering, automatic control, and physiology – fields that traditionally were considered widely apart and having no relations with each other at all. This in itself is a significant achievement, because progress in fields that today are of great importance to the well-being of mankind, such as urban renewal and water and air purification, heavily depends on interdisciplinary work. The space program proves that such work is possible on a truly grand scale, and it teaches how one must proceed.

Oh yes, I forgot to mention computers. I wanted to save them up, for the following reason: Space travel has been a particularly intriguing subject to science-fiction writers for many decades. They have described all possible aspects of space in great detail long ago. And if we look through the works of the very early authors like Jules Verne, or – perhaps better known to German readers – Kurt Lasswitz, we can only admire the accuracy with which they were able to predict the overall systems aspects as well as many details – with one great exception: The need of computers. In the eyes of the early science-fiction writers, space travels could be managed with relatively simple calculations, often even of an algebraic rather than numerical nature. Today of course we know how indispensable digital computers are in space travel. Their importance goes far beyond making mere numerical calculations. In fact, if we analyze interdisciplinary relationship, it is probably fair to say that computer technology crossed the boundary lines of more disciplines than any other. In Apollo 11, more than 600 computers were required to get the astronauts to the moon and back. And these machines were not stand-alone units – they were part of one single, immensely complex system. It is quite possible that the future phases of the space race will not be determined by the thrust of the rockets, but by the ability to manage huge computer systems.

Computers thus are an instrumental element in space. But the converse holds true here too: Space is having a significant impact on computer development. The requirements for ultra-high reliability and – in the case of spaceborne systems – low weight have placed a tremendous pressure on engineers to devise solutions which previously were considered impossible. Man–machine interaction through display consoles and other devices has been greatly advanced. And, perhaps most important of all, the needs of space technology have caused the theory of automatic control to be enriched by some new chapters of fundamental importance and very general applicability.

Computers and power

Let me now shift to an entirely different field of computer use: Computers and power. By "power" I do not mean political, military or industrial strength – I mean the generation and distribution of electric power, one of the basic resources of any modern civilisation. Why, among all fields, am I going to dwell upon this? There is a very special, a personal reason, and I beg you to forgive a past president of IFIP to talk about himself at least for a few seconds: For 18 years I have devoted all my working hours (and some of the non-working time as well) to computers. I have done research, development, teaching, writing, and I have contributed my share to professional society activities. After so much time I felt I ought to do something entirely different, and I decided to move into an environment whose main involvement is in the generation and the distribution of electric power.

It is a common saying that the fields of computers and of power are on the opposite ends of the scale of innovation dynamics. Even business school textbooks say that computers are progressive, fast moving, dynamic, highly competitive, whereas the power field allegedly is conservative, slowly moving, and only mildly competitive. Let yourselves be advised by someone who by now has an intimate inside knowledge of both areas: This is oversimplified and largely incorrect. This kind of judgement is made by people who are reasonably well-acquainted with computers, but who have not bothered to study the power field in any depth.

It is often said that computers are the most complex mechanisms devised and built by humans, and I am convinced that this statement is correct. Next in the scale of complexity we probably find communication networks, closely followed by power networks. A power system is a vastly complicated network with interrelations which are based on laws and principles which today are only partially understood. It is necessary to move towards a much deeper understanding of these relations for the following reason: Highly industrialised regions today expect a service from their power suppliers of a kind that computer users normally cannot get: 100% availability, 24 hours a day, 365 days a year. It takes a large amount of controlled redundancy and error-correcting mechanisms to assure this.

As far as the degree of industrial competitiveness in the power field and the computer field is concerned, I should only like to mention that competitive pressures have forced manufacturers of power plants in some cases to guarantee the refund of *full consequential damages in the case of equipment failure*, and the magnitude of this liability is unlimited. This is a condition to which computer companies would never agree. And, the risks involved are not trivial, considering that a large power plant costs ten times as much as even the largest computer.

But direct relations now start to develop between computers and power systems. The widely publicised blackout which in 1965 deprived the entire North-East of the United States of power for several hours was an alarm sign. The sequence of events which led to the disaster has been reconstructed with great accuracy. In the course of these studies it was learned that in systems of this high degree of complexity there can occur conditions of instability, even under perfectly normal operating circumstances, in which an almost arbitrarily small perturbation can have catastrophic effects. Clearly such conditions must be avoided, and it is computer control which will supply the remedy. Power companies have long resisted the introduction of computers within their systems, because computer manufacturers would not provide adequate assurance for reliability and availability. This has now changed; improved systems design is providing the needed margins of safety.

But what is needed is not only computer hardware. In fact, the machines currently envisaged in power systems are small or at most medium in size. What must now be obtained is a better systems understanding and a systematic application of the modern tools of control theory – the tools developed for space travel. It is interesting and highly significant that the electrical engineering department at M.I.T. is currently strengthening its research activities in power systems, and that the group doing this work is largely staffed by people who have grown up not in power systems, but in space technology.

Hardware versus software

Those among us who were in the computer field from the early days find it startling in retrospect to dwell on the changing relations between hardware and software. In the very early times, these two concepts were not clearly separated at all. Hardware and software were often done by the same people and were treated in the same publications. A lecture on computers might have included, within less than an hour, a flip-flop circuit, a numerical method, and the description of a flow diagram. This of course soon changed, and in the course of the separation of the two disciplines one thing is well worth mentioning: Productivity and progress, as well as the interest of technical people seemed to be focused on hardware in the 1950's, on software in the 1960's – at least this is the impression one gets if one reads through journals and conference proceedings. This is evidence of the fact that hardware had reached a certain maturity by 1960 and thereafter advanced more in degree than in principle. Software, on the other hand, started to reap the fruits of the most important idea conceived in the '50's, which is programming languages. The dichotomy of hardware and software has a striking and very amusing analogy in one of the arts, namely in music: Hardware is represented by the musical instruments, software by the compositions. It is a most exhilarating task to meditate on the relations between musical hardware and software in the light of history and to draw parallels with computers. The time scales in the process of historical evolution of course are different by a factor of 10 or even 100.

IFIP came into being 10 years ago, and it is a credit to the wisdom and foresight of its founders that, right from the beginning, they decided to concentrate on systems and software aspects. These men rightly concluded that great and important advances were to come in these fields. Progress in hardware remained of vital importance, to be sure; but it was recognised that the existing electrical and electronics engineering societies were well equipped to handle professional society life in the components and devices field. At IFIP congresses, hardware aspects therefore were limited to survey sessions. Thus, the theme of my talk, Computers and Technology, has never been a primary concern of IFIP. The events of the past 10 years have amply proved how right this ground rule has been.

On the intelligent use of computers

The total computing power of all computers installed today, expressed in operations per second, is almost incredibly high. It probably exceeds 10^9 operations per second. This is 10 times more than would be produced if the entire population of the world – men, women and children – were calculating intensely, each one with a personal desk-top calculator. A question is justified, which was hardly in order 10 years ago, let alone 20 years ago: Whether all this fantastic computational power is used intelligently. The answer plainly is NO: Parts are used intelligently, but not all. Perhaps the question itself is not very profound: If someone were to ask whether all of the 10^8 automobiles in the world were used for intelligent purposes, everybody would without hesitation give him the answer NO. But I believe computers are different: the unintelligent ways in which they can be used are worse than in the case of other technical tools. Many people are rightly concerned that their private lives are becoming invaded and their financial integrity even endangered by computers. Danger lies not so much in the central processor, but in the input-output devices. I am of course expressing a platitude if I say that computers themselves are neither good nor evil. It is a little less trivial to say that with these tools irresponsible people can act a lot more irresponsibly than without. A striking example is the fact that currently millions of credit cards are being distributed to men, women and even children who do not want them, do not need them and have not asked for them, thus exposing them to financial risks beyond their means. Clearly, without computers such peculiar action would be impossible.

But even scientific computer users – in other words, people who should be trained to think analytically and to deploy their research tools rationally – often do not apply the best of taste in solving their problems by machines. This is especially so in those cases where a desired scientific result can be obtained in three different ways: By physical measurement, by analytical reasoning, or by calculation. All too often, calculation is chosen indiscriminately, even in those cases where an experiment would be less costly. Further, we all know that many computer programs are far from optimal – in fact, some are very wasteful indeed. As a result many a research director occasionally feels compelled to remind his scientists to do a little less computing and a little more thinking. This need is most likely to arise in a research institution where computing time is provided free of charge, in other words, where the cost of computing is not added to the total project cost. In this case, the criteria for choice of the right research tool get quite distorted, which is not in the best interest of scientific progress.

Finally, let me say a few words about the relations between computers and society. We currently live in an age in which almost all human and social standards, even those that were thought to be proven valid over many centuries, are being challenged. Technical progress itself, hitherto considered overwhelmingly beneficial, is now coming under attack. As a result we witness an increasing alienation between large segments of the population and technology. This alienation has a strong emotional content, and all too often the computer is the object around which the emotions crystallize. Unfortunately computer users themselves have supplied their opponents with reasons for complaint occasionally. I believe IFIP can pride itself of the fact that its people have always acted as highly responsible members of the computer community. I also believe IFIP has an important, a vitally important task facing itself: To address itself to the problems surrounding the relations between computers and society. This should probably be done not so much with an organised undertaking such as a working group, but rather with a concerted effort on the part of all people associated with IFIP to act as responsible citizens and educators within their countries and to assure whenever or wherever they can, that the population understands and appreciates computers. It may well be that the orderly progress in computers in the future will depend more on the proper handling of these problems than on further advances in hardware and software.

ADMINISTRATION AND COMPUTERISED INFORMATION SYSTEMS

by

D. CHEVION

Jerusalem

Amongst the many fields of application of computers, administration seems to be one of the most difficult. Although tens of thousands of computers are employed in the field of administration, it can hardly be said that the difficulties have been settled during the last decade. We are overwhelmed with problems which are not only very complicated from the theoretical point of view but which are also very, very costly. There is thus an incentive to talk frankly on this topic and, especially justified, is that it be done here while we are among ourselves.

How many "sweet dreams" have perished about the use of computers in the field of administration? How many disappointments have there been? There is hardly a field where the disappointments have been so large; the promises and the expectations were, in general, by far larger than the practical achievements.

The knowledge of the real possibilities of the "black box" will enable us to look into the future; being much safer and better equipped. This will assist us in seeing how far it is in fact possible to computerise information systems in administration.

Neglection of administration in the early time

The application of computers in administration has been pursued by an "original sin", from the very first day of the existence of computers.

Computers were not originally devised to solve problems of administration. Even such outstanding computer pioneers as A.M. Turing did not think that administration was a suitable branch of thought for the machine to exercise its power. When speaking about the possibility of producing a thinking machine he says "we propose to try and see what can be done with a brain which is more or less without a body, provided with organs of sight, speech and hearing. We have been faced with the problem of finding suitable processes of thought for the machine to put its power in. The following findings appear to me to have advantages: various games, e.g. chess, bridge, poker, the learning of languages, translation of languages, cryptography and mathematics".

Administration thus has not been mentioned nor taken into account. This "original sin" which for a long time was felt both in the hardware and software domain is still in existence. Although administration is now the widest field of application it belongs to the "youngest". It is not astonishing that mutual adaptation of administration and computers is a source of many difficulties.

Administration as a man-computer interrelationship

In all our systems, in whatever field, we are faced with the man-computer interrelationship. In administration, however, this man-computer interrelationship is of a basic nature. One may say generally that in each administrative system human beings, organised around tools, machines or computers, strive to attain by that means prescribed aims and to perform certain functions. This is the most general way to look at a system which deals with administration. It is well-known how many problems arose from human relations within a system, the more we have to expect by encountering a new family of relations, namely, the relationship between the physical entity and the human being. The relative share of the two elements in the man-machine system of administration depends on the development of that system. While in the most primitive set-up the system is just a man, in the more advanced system, the man element will be brought to a minimum. The total elimination of man from that partnership exists only – we feel – in an ideal model to which one comes closer; closer but not to be regarded as a practical possibility. There are various reasons for this: technical, human, sociological, etc.

In analysing the problem we might look at our administration system also from a different point of view, namely a system composed of three main functions: input, processing and output. We consider such a triangle as a basic system and may compose, out of it, composed systems of various size. Actually, each system can be looked upon from different angles: on one side, as a basic system, and on the other, as a composed one. We can hardly talk about basic systems of administration without being able to divide them into more basic units.

The chain of systems, from the more complicated ones to the simplest one, is thus an endless one, open on both sides. Similarly to problems of matter, if the composed system becomes too complicated it falls apart. Whether an upper limit does exist can hardly be predicted. The use of computers in administration should be analysed from two points of view:
(A) The functioning of a simple so to say "atomic system",
(B) The functioning of the composed system.

Basic systems

Let's begin with the Basic System:

Input – The system depends on the input of data whatever they are: characters, numbers, symbols – all that is to be processed.

If instead of movement of physical entities containing the information, the information itself will enter directly into the processing unit of the system, this will not only save time and ensure the highest possible accuracy, but eliminate the existence of translation media. Costs of transmission are lower than have been the costs of the movement of physical entities containing the information. Automated basic systems depend on how far the input can be automated. The problems encountered here are more of a technical character, but some transgress the technical limits and point to deeper and tougher problems which cannot be solved easily in the immediate future. The key for this is of course pattern recognition of any technique available. Any constraint still existing in pattern recognition limits the possibility of elimination of men's intelligences. Is it possible in the foreseeable future to attain standardisation of symbols and forms of data? Any deviation from the standard will make the interaction of men's intelligence inevitable.

Output – Input and output are certainly relative notions and the same output can serve another basic system as input or vice versa.

The problems with respect to output are more or less similar to those of input; they are even simpler because here we do not face the difficulty of pattern recognition, as output is already properly prepared in the computer. From that point of view, the output is already standardised without imposing on it any substantial constraint. What happens, however, if a change in output becomes necessary? Even if that change is not connected with the collection of new data, reprogramming is required. Flexibility of output is thus limited by the degree of automatic programming; a problem which brings us into considerations connected with the processing.

Processing – This is the main problem. Processing in administration is composed of many operations. For instance: planning, designing, creating, classifying, sorting, calculating, recording, and decision making. What are the principles which enable the information handling processes to be formalised in the language understandable to a computer and fully eliminate human intervention?

Representation of data

Operations with data which carry information depend first of all on the possibility of physical representation of that data. The quantifiability of such representation enables us to determine the order which is the basis for operations such as sorting, classifying, etc. Non-quantifiable physical representation can be ordered only by enumeration; such a procedure lacks of course the advantages of an analytical principle by means of which automated handling can be performed. Handling is here well understood in the most general way, namely both physical manipulation of data only (recording) and processing (calculation, logical operations). It is quite clear that not all data which appear in the vocabulary of an administrative system have a quantifiable physical representation and, as a consequence of that, we are confronted with a limit for automation which is, in the main, of a principal character.

Rules of inference – Principles of processing

However, this is only part of the problem. Processing within the basic administrative system means also planning, creating and decision making. How about that? The processing here means the acceptance of certain statements on the basis of other statements already accepted. We look then for clear rules of inference. An interesting feature is revealed again: as long as these rules have a deductive, clearly specified character they can well be formalised within the computer programming language. However, if either of the following cases takes place, an automated decision process cannot materialise.

(A) Not all statements which form the assumption for the inference are known or even cannot be known beforehand. The class of these statements is simply not complete and its completion depends on circumstances which cannot be programmed in advance.

(B) All statements are given, however, the *inference rules* are not known or are of a non-deductive character and based on probabilistic considerations.

The higher the decision process is, the more it is unclear what actually are the relevant considerations (statements) required and what weight should be attached to each consideration. Subjective factors overshadow here the picture of the objectivity required for processing without ad hoc human intervention.

We thus face a limit for automation which has a principal character. This, however, does not mean that all decision processes cannot be incorporated into a computerised system. Firstly, the majority of decision making does not fall under the above high class. The rules of inference and the assumption statements are generally quite simple and, after succeeding to collect the data (which is a *real* problem but not of a principal character), it is easy to devise within the automated system the chain of considerations which lead to conclusions on the basis of an accepted algorithm.

Also, in cases in which it seems that decision making could hardly be formalised, it turns out to be the opposite after a considerable amount of analysis and investigation into the detailed process. Modern scientific methods of operations research and simulation play a major part in that analysis and have contributed to the fact that many, many decisions previously regarded as non-deductive, subjective and based on imponderable elements have upon closer scrutiny, turned to be objective and quantifiable or at least could have been represented adequately by using the capabilities of the computer. A simplified example of the decision process in the reorder of commodity in an inventory may serve as an illustration.

The reordering functions performed by man could have been looked upon as a judgement of the specialist to meet the situation according to the data which he has on hand based on previous experience aquired. If he is a qualified man with a good professional institution, he might in many cases make correct reorder decisions without being conscious how he reaches that decision and without being able to explain it to another person. However, operations research techniques, based on good data influx about commodity utilization in the past, on plans for future requirements, on knowledge about economical data trends, prices etc., and finally, on data about the physical characteristics of the commodity, (deterioration, obsolescence) can almost completely formalize this decision process and eliminate thus the necessity of human intervention.

Many similar cases in the decision process in the administration field have been formalized or can be formalized by means of techniques which use statistical methods, operations research, and simulation – and thus including all that into the program of the processing unit. It is quite clear that such functions, like sorting, recording, calculating, can of course be programmed and all the decisions connected with such functions are thus automated. However, it seems clear that it is hard to foresee that all decision processes can be formalized in an adequate computer language. It is hardly to be assumed that a decision regarding the depreciation of an exchange rate could be programmed even if we could assume that all data which are required would be available. The logic of the decision in such a case or in a similar one, even if we will not take into account external pressures and contradictory interests – which of course cannot be formalized, – even in such a case the major factors for the decision have a probabilistic character, and the weight which has to be attributed to the various factors, can hardly be objectively established.

It seems to be one of the major challenges of the future to discover the types of inference techniques used and the various decision processes in the administration in order to be able to simulate as many as possible of them, by an objective process which can be formalized in a computer language.

So far with the main problems of the basic system; let's now proceed to the composite one, namely a system which is composed of two or more basic systems.

Composite systems

The models of composition, in other words the architecture of the system represent the levels of integration which is one of the main trends in the construction of systems of administration. The degree of integration is measuring the degree of automation a composed system is able to achieve.

First model: the basic systems operate completely independently. However, for the input: all common data or at least part of them are *compatible* and/or capable of comparison. Although this is relatively quite a low degree of integration. Nevertheless, its great usefulness to management is clearly detected when considering the possibility of independent outputs which can be compared and utilised for more advanced decision making. The question arises whether and how compatibility of data of independent systems can be achieved and, further, how it can be maintained. Thus already at the lowest model of systems architecture we are faced with a principal problem.

Second model: the basic systems operate independently; however, the output of one, or at least part of it, serves as input to the second. Such a model of integration secures the maintenance; the continued existence of the compatibility, but still leaves unresolved the problems connected with it.

Third model: we might consider a model in which all data currently originating or within a data bank enter into a common processing unit, wherefrom separate outputs for each of the systems participating in that model are produced. This is of course a very high level of integration.

There are innumerable variations in the architecture of composition; we will, however, for the purpose of this paper, satisfy ourselves with the three models mentioned above.

Compatibility and identification

Integration implies that there are common notions in the language of each of the systems. The ideal case where the language in all possible systems is one and the same is simply impossible, because the language used in the administration, although it is the same natural language by name, is far from being the same language according to semantic meaning. The ambiguity originates in the ambiguity of the natural language itself and cannot be avoided unless we construct a special artificial language for the administration and ensure that all the similar words contained in it have, in fact, the same meaning. Construction of a common language in administration or at least, devising parts of it, is principally the main pre-requisite for the possibility of integration as such, at any level. This is a great task for the future. However, in the meantime, we have to satisfy ourselves with partial achievements. Let us take an example. The word "family" has a different meaning when used in a statistical administrative context; a different one in a social-security file and, further, a different one in the population register.

There are still numerous other administrative languages in which the word "family" appears and has again different meanings.

Integration of systems, at any level, which use the word "family" depends on the possibility to break up the notion into elements in order to enable further their *modular* build-up according to the variety of meanings required. This is not always possible and, at least, not easy. The modular construction of common notions in different systems from well-defined elements is a principal condition for integration and it leads often, even in a successful case, to a cumbersome and complicated method in systems design, programming and processing. A quite substantive *payment* sacrificed to the "God of Integration" or the "God of MIS" as one might like to put it.

However, that is not enough. Another real principal problem is *identification.* Administrative systems deal with objects: persons, land, cars, commodities etc. Integration implies that there exists some one-to-one correlation between the name used in the computer and its designate. In the ideal case it is one and the same system of identification. Unless it is an ideal case, it is again built out of modular structure and applied differently in different systems but capable of reciprocal one-to-one translation. The common identification procedure is again not always possible, surely not always easy; it leads to more complications as it compels in many cases the use, in a simple system-language, of a very complicated identification method suitable in fact to another far more advanced system to which, however, the simple system is linked.

Techniques

So much for compatibility and identification barriers for integration concerning the language used in the system. What about the techniques? The coordination and compatibility seems in that respect not to submit difficulties of a principal character. Compatibility among computers is achievable, although against heavy costs in money and effectiveness.

One would accept as understandable the impossibility of standardising the natural language; however, what about the hardware and software? Can we not expect to set standards here to enable compatibility at low cost and at easy effort? Practically speaking this should have been the situation; however, it deviates to not a small extent from that.

In spite of the inherent difficulties in attaining compatibility standards in the technical field and to maintain them, it might be said to be quite conclusive that techniques are striving towards more and more effective back-up for integration, for the functioning of composed administrative information systems.

Finally, what about the architecture of composition itself? We have enumerated various models of integration; innumerably more variations exist in reality. Are there rules for such an architecture? Is there a limit to its structure? Have we to count with an optimum size, or an optimum number of systems brought together in such a way or another under one roof?

The reply to that question depends again on factors, part of which are of a transitional character and will vanish in time; some carry a principal bearing and seem to point towards limits beyond which automation of elementary and composed administrative systems cannot develop.

Technical factors – economic advantages in scale of large computers, their growing rate of compatibility in software and hardware, development of sophisticated operation systems, telecommunications, and on-line techniques of various natures point towards the clear conclusion that techniques are and will also in the future be a positive momentum towards higher and higher integration and deeper and deeper automation. One might say that technically we have no barriers of a principal nature; however, economic considerations and the availability of adequate manpower are actually controlling the situation.

Large-scale memories, at constantly decreasing cost, provide an excellent technical solution for huge data banks, while the growing speed of CPU enables access to data at a rate which hardly proves critical in the majority of administrative systems. It is now neither the memory nor the time which are the critical elements to the establishment of integrated management systems. The critical path has in fact moved from the technical arena to factors of a different character.

Architecture of integrated systems

Systems design – are there rules for the architecture of automated integrated systems? If such rules exist they would have to be developed within the science of administration and management, whether public or private. Such rules, as far as they exist apparently follow some guiding principles which have been developed in the mathematical-logical approach. Theoretically we would like – assuming for a moment that all principal problems regarding decision making, compatibility of language and identification, are not a real obstacle – to integrate as many systems as possible; ideally speaking we strive towards one huge data bank with all data passing through a common "black-box" which will provide all outputs required in the administrative systems of a society.

This principle of maximisation is, however, curbed seriously by a number of other guidelines, namely: simplicity, effectiveness, flexibility and cost. None of them can, at the present moment, be sufficiently quantified and measured in an objective manner.

Do computerised integrated systems have an optimum size? Definitely, yes, but this size is itself dependent on many variables which develop and change. Administrative systems have to perform some function according to prevailing conditions. These conditions change; it is then that the time for the establishment of an integrated system has not to surpass certain limits. Otherwise, we will face the awkward situation where the perfectly established system turns out to be useless in practice. Such cases have happened and it is more than true to say that along with the time factor, the best is the greatest enemy of the good. Maximization was perfect, however, ineffective.

The same relation exists also between maximization and the remainder of the guidelines. Maximization has thus its break-even point beyond of which it turns to influence the structure of systems in a negative way.

To know where this point is, is *the* real merit of the system designer. In spite of many objective yardsticks – especially in the field of cost, manpower and time calculations – it is basically a subjective sense of proportion; a pragmatic feeling of what is the optimal possibility in view of the prevailing circumstances and a forecast of their change in the future. We face here another limit of a principal nature for integration. However, not a static limit, but a dynamic one which changes with the conditions determining simplicity, effectiveness, flexibility and cost.

Main factors determining the depth of automation and the size of integration

Data banks

Let's look now at the immense data banks which are, of course, a prerequisite of integrated systems; is really such a concentration of information required? The growing amount of information collected and stored for eventual use places the user in a real trap; integration and automation means storage of data. Abundance creates a burden and then the whole system tends to become ineffective and costly. What is really needed is selected and significant information; however, this cannot be achieved by automated and integrated systems themselves: the interaction of human intelligence seems to be required here; thus again a limit of principal character towards full automation is worth remembering.

Centralisation – decentralisation

Automated integrated systems mean in fact centralisation – another point which creates difficulties in the design, implementation and operation of the system. Each organisation has its critical mass of centralisation beyond which it endangers its existence. While in the manual administration a trend towards delegation of power, decisions and decentralisation has definitely taken place, the automated systems tend seemingly to revert this development.

This is only partly true as telecommunications and on-line processing enable most distant points in the organisation to act independently and allow them a degree of freedom which is larger than that in a conventional set-up. Yet, in spite of all that, the tension between centralisation and decentralisation no doubt exists and acts as a curb on the trend towards integration.

This is not a limiting factor of principal character; however, being partly organisational and partly human it is hardly to be assumed that its influence will be lessened in the near future.

Other organisational aspects

Integration means to adjust the organisation of an office to new rhythms, to new relationships. This is not an easy task. Computers call for adaptation of offices to a new environment and this cannot be achieved without far-reaching changes. Integration multiplies the need for such adaptation, thus it confronts a difficulty of a transitional character and of a very stubborn nature. Haste towards integration may be here detrimental and adds a strongly limiting factor.

Flexibility

Automated decision processes impair, according to the present state of development, the degree of flexibility. Whereas the conventional human decision process could swiftly undergo change. This is hardly the case when reprogramming is required – a relatively time-consuming activity. Integration adds even more rigidity and obstinacy towards changes. Automatic systems design and programming might be of some help to lessen the rigidity; however, we are as yet still far away from the possibility of counting on this in the operative way. The degree of flexibility required from the system limits thus its degree of automation and integration; once again we face here a limiting factor of principal character, unless automatic programming becomes a real possibility.

Human factors

The men in the system determine its automation and integration. Conservative approaches fear change; fear to accept not conventionally readable documents, and insufficient or even no knowledge at all in information processing are among the greatest enemies of automation. All that can change and no doubt will do so in the future; however, the speed of change is far too small. Moreover, we need a completely new generation of managers and decision-makers. It must be a generation which is able to face the probabilistic approach where some problems have no single solution and several options have to be considered.

Automated and integrated administration systems postulate the existence of proper reserves of managerial and professional manpower. Is it too much to expect that first-generation people manage fourth-generation computers?

Here again a limit of extreme deterrent influence and long-term character in spite of its – so we believe – intrinsic transitional nature.

Sociological factors

Also sociological factors strongly influence systems and design and its philosophy. Fear to lose personal freedom and privacy is the moving force against integration and data-banks; although the gist of the problem does not lie in systems design (can we really believe that system designers like Plato's philosophers will rule the world!), but in the constitutional structure and the regime of each country, we nevertheless cannot disregard the strong influence this belief has on integration; one might certainly prefer to live in a computerised but democratic society and not in a manually organized and dictatorial one; this shows no doubt where the kernel of the problem is. In spite of that it seems today still impossible to enfore hastily data-banks and integration beyond a certain accepted degree, depending on conditions in each separate country. Again, a limiting factor for system-design, a very, very mighty one, not, however, of a lasting character. The eventual danger of automation will hopefully in the future be curbed by proper laws and regulations embedded in the regime of the relevant country; thus automation itself will be free to develop undisturbed within the framework of such arrangements.

Cost

Finally, the cost is the most objective element regulating integration in particular and systems design in general. In view of so many non-measurable factors – some encouraging, the other curbing the establishment of an automated management system – special importance is attached to the problem of cost. This is a very efficient regulator, actually the strongest one which determines the degree of integration and automation to be pursued. Although the value of some advantages of a new system cannot be simply expressed in terms of money (e.g. better service to the public) or cannot be well estimated, we may, by all means, consider the financial outlay as a limiting factor; however, of a non-principal character. The break-even point for acceptance or rejection of a system depends on quite a number of parameters which frequently change; the limit is thus not a static one; it is dynamic and should be constantly revised.

We have now reached the end of the enumeration of the main factors which determine both the depth of automation and the size of integration of computerised administrative information systems. When applying computers to administration we face a quite specific situation. The peculiarity is not limited only to historical reasons mentioned already at the beginning: in the majority of cases, the science of the field of applications, be it mathematics, physics, chemistry or economy, existed long before the computer entered the arena of history. Different situations exist with regard to administration and management; the very fervent development of scientific, systematic thinking took place actually concurrently with the development of computer philosophy and technique.

This is a very important feature.

Computers have participated in the development of the science of systems administration; more rules and principles have been shaped by them, than has been found to have existed before the era of automation. Computer philosophy is already interwoven in basic thoughts on administration and will continue to be the "spiritus movens" of that discipline. The very fact that there did not exist before computers being applied to administration, a clear shape of a scientific structure in that field is a major source of difficulties and misconceptions about the rules of computer implementation, their power and limits. So it has happened that computers and computer philosophy form a part of the science of administrative systems. History cannot be now turned back and in all future theoretical developments in the science of administration, this fact has to be borne in mind.

Conclusions

Whatever the outcome of this theoretical development, it is already clear that there are principal limits for the elimination of human intelligence from administrative systems. Three of them are of foremost importance, namely:

Probabilistic reasoning, compatibility of semantic meaning of words, and modular systems of identification

As to integration and systems architecture, although technically the limitations seem to be vanishing more and more, we face barriers originating from human, sociological and economical sources. The limits and the barriers are not rigid. Although they exist they can be moved and pushed away with the development of society and the education of its managerial strata. Thus here again the principle of modularity has to be applied. Similar to modules in building up the definition of a basic administrative vocabulary, composed administration systems have to be structured of independent modular units, capable – if in future development, time and money allow and human understanding ripens – of being set together to form one piece. Modularity is the best theoretical weapon to get, on one hand, partial systems working as fast as possible – thus securing effectiveness and, on the other hand, to be prepared for future expansion and improvement without extensive investments in redesign and reprogramming.

Our success in following that path depends to a large extent on the fast development of rules and principles within the science of administration systems. One should not bypass here the extremely important role in this development played by the public sector of administration in general and of governments in particular. There is hardly a field where theory and practice are so much interrelated. The active attitude of governments in fostering computer education, computer research and implementation of computerised administration systems is of foremost importance. We can hardly assume a real step forward without the conscious enhancement which will be given to that field by the public sector. In fact all achievements till now are due to investment on behalf of governments and this has to be so to a large extent in the future. The skill to design a well-computerised administration system is also of paramount importance to developing countries; let's not dwell now on the theoretical problem whether the gap between developed and developing countries is closing or not. It should be clear that the necessary – may be not sufficient – conditions for achieving this are the acquisition of skills of *modularity* in building computerised systems. Such a modular approach towards small and developing countries may have advantages; a merit be fully and speedily exploited.

Fully automated and integrated administration systems are, for various principal reasons, not to be attained. However, the room between the achievements of to-day and the dynamic limits of tomorrow is still extremely large for challenges of immense advance.

Telecommunications and on-line processing have brought about the "squeeze" of time and space in administration systems. Simultaneous events can be simultaneously processed and occurrences in the same system can be controlled and managed from one spot. The possibility to overcome time intervals and space distances supply the systems designer with a weapon of outstanding effectiveness. Decision making, although highly probabilistic in the higher sphere, can be assisted extraordinarily here. It has been for instance found experimentally that technical devices, in spite of their not being able to fully replace the human decision process, can improve it substantially. Lately, experiments with graphic displays have proven that statement anew.

The theoretical limits disillusion us of dreams and, so good, but carry with them the profound message that further advance in computerisation of administration is possible and in fact indispensable. They carry also the optimistic message that in the man-computer partnership, man's share has to be strengthened. The men to remain the master and the Prague-Golem Legend may be here a real memento.

Is the share of men in decision making new? No!

More than 2000 years ago we can read in the metaphysics of Aristotle the following astonishing truth: "Effectiveness of an army depends on the order and its commander, but mainly on the latter because he is not depending on the order, whereas the order is depending on him".

FROM SCIENTIFIC COMPUTATION TO COMPUTER SCIENCE

by

F. L. BAUER
Munich

Our century is generally believed to be the century of science. Science is everywhere – public media propagate it, and the typical advertisement does not fail to mention "this is scientific proof". This century has had already more scientists than any of the previous ones, and has seen more scientific publications than all the earlier ones together. Nevertheless, science is not an invention of our days. It is as old as our cultures are; it is a companion of any culture.

To count is an achievement of Man, a relatively recent one of the *homo sapiens*. Independent cultures have developed it independently, as we know from number systems that go along with counting. The observation of the sky leads to counting the days between new moon, the days between the equinoxes. As the sky is the realm of the Gods, counting acquires a divine aspect, numbers are mystical symbols. A word that has been cited frequently with a wrong connotation, Kronecker's famous "Die ganzen Zahlen hat Gott geschaffen... ", belongs to this circle. In Babylon, in the Pythagorean school, with the Aztecs, counting forms, due to its ritual importance, an essential part of the culture. Counting also has practical aspects. Coins and a monetary system, chronology and geometry are the forerunners of mathematical sciences. Quite soon, Man discovers that counting and computation are hard work. To make it possible, to make it simpler becomes a matter of skill. Computation as such becomes science. This was still the situation in the 16th century, when Adam Riese taught a wide public how to calculate "on the lines and with the feather", the latter being the new art, using digits instead of calculi. It was the time, when the university of Altdorf near Nuremberg attracted students with the promise that they could even learn how to divide. Not from the universities, but from the comptoirs of the trade house, basically from Italy, comes the ⟨arte de la mercadantia⟩.

Fig. 1. Title page of Adam Riese's second arithmetic book, 1529 edition.

However, it was the beginning of the Modern Times. Within a few decades, we see Galilei, Kepler, Descartes, Huygens, Newton. A new era of the natural sciences arrives, and it is characterized by quantitative theory. Scientific computation in a broad sense enters the picture.

The liberation of Man from the burden of monotonous mental labour

Calculating was still hard work. And despite the fact that the computations of algebra were done with letters, that the newly invented Calculus dealt with "indivisibles", calculations with numbers became necessary at a much increased scale. One would expect that these tiring computations would have given rise to the first calculating machines.

We know little about the motivation of Schickart (1592–1635), who built such a machine first in 1623. But for Pascal, born in 1623, who invented at the age of 19 his calculating machine, the incentive was the desire to simplify the accounting work he had to do for his father, who was a tax collector at Rouen.

It was not so much the need to perform voluminous scientific computation that gave rise to the first calculating machine, it was the goal to liberate Man from the burden of monotonous labour, or, more profanely, it was the laziness of Man. We should not overlook this if we are in danger of overemphasizing the dignity of our field.

Scientific computation plays an important role in the next centuries. It is the usual companion of applied mathematics – an indispensable tool of physics, astronomy, geodesy. This is nowhere better seen than in the life of Gauss – this eminent mathematician did not hesitate to do an enormous amount of computational work all by himself.

"Compute" and "calculate"

Going back again in history, I would like to draw your attention to the origin of the words "*calculate*" and "*compute*". In ancient Latin, calculi were the stones used in the Roman abacus. The word, originating from lat. *calx,* pebble, was used to denote objects from stone, bone, metal, glass. In the 13th century, in France, the calculi are called jetons (Engl. *counter,* Germ. *Rechenpfennig,* Netherl. *leggelt*); they

Fig. 2. Counting board *and* casting counter. Pythagoras (right) before a *casting counter* with the numbers 1241 and 82; Boethius (left) before Indian numerals. From the "Margita Philosophica" by the Carthusian prior Gregor Reisch, 1503.

are coined and show symbols, usually of the sovereign. The board on which they are moved along lines is the *bureau* (Engl. *counter, cownter,* Germ. *Rechenbrett,* Netherl. *kunttore*). The French Revolution makes counters and calculi disappear in France and all over Europe, but the abacus is still in use, the Japanese *soroban*, the Chinese *suanpan*, the Russian *stschjoty*. And *calculare*, the term that came up in mediaeval Latin, has penetrated into many languages. German *rechnen,* Netherl. *reken*, Engl. *reckon*, to get (the stones) in order (straight), Greek ψηφιζειν are direct counterparts.

By the way, the ancient Romans knew well to differentiate between the *calculatores* and the *arenarii,* the geometers that drew pictures in the sand, and whereas a calculator obtained 75 denares for teaching, an arenarius got 200 denares.

In mediaeval Latin, *computus* is a calendar computation. It is derived from Lat. *putare,* to cut (*kerben*), *imputare* meant

Fig. 3. The oldest French *counters* (13th century); 20 mm diameter.

Fig. 4. *Counting table* with labeled *counter-strips.*

Fig. 5. *Counters.* The "Nurnberg school pennies" (above); with a *chequered cloth* (above right). Below: Venice's winged lion (left), the reverse side of the second above with alphabet, the German *counter* from 1691 (right).

to cut something on the tally, *deputare,* to cut off something from the tally. Engl. *to compute*, Fr. *compter* have this origin. The tally, Lat. *talea,* It. *taglia,* Fr. *taille,* Germ. *Kerbholz,* Netherl. *Kerfstock,* Bav. *Raitholz,* Rhaet. *stiala,* Alem. *Tessel,* Sl. *rovaš* was also discovered in China, 2000 years old, near the Great Wall.

From the cuts in the tally, our Roman number symbols originated. Thus, computing means, strictly speaking, to count and to compute with the help of number symbols, and calculating means, strictly speaking, to calculate with the help of an abacus or with calculi on the lines. None of the two refers directly to our modern radix notation, to the use of figure symbols. This system and the figure symbols both originated in India, some centuries before or after Christ. The essential step was made by the invention of the zero, the Indian *sunya*, empty, that was translated into Arabian *as-sifr,* from which Fr. *chiffre,* Germ. *Ziffer,* Engl. *cipher* comes with the meaning of *figure, numeral, digit* as well as of a secret code. But in parallel, *as-sifr* changed through the Italian *zefiro, zevero, zero* to French and English *zéro, zero.* The German *Null* is derived from nulla, in *nulla figura,* no (essential) figure. But independently, we find a radix notation in the Maya Calendar.

A man from what is today Uzbekistan, Muhammed ibn Musa al-Chwarizmi, around 820 after Christ, described the new number system in a book, that was translated into Latin and copied in the early 12th century. This marks the begin of the victory of the radix notation and the corresponding calculation. Leonardo di Pisa states in 1202 *Sed hoc totum quasi errorem computavi respectu modi Indorum* ('But all this is to be considered erroneous compared with the method of the Indians').

Rightfully, the new art is called *Algorismus,* and in the beginning of the 16th century, the struggle against the *abacists* starts in middle Europe. The calculating machines of Schickart, Pascal, Leibniz, are based on the radix notation, and historically we should call our field Algorithmia.

Fig. 6. An *abacist* and an *algorithmist.* From a book on the seven liberal arts by Robert Recorde, physician in ordinary to the king.

Accordingly, Algorithm can be interpreted as doing a computation with numbers by handling their figures in a radix notation. The division algorithm with figures is in fact very similar to the division algorithm for polynomials. It is this latter and wider use that characterizes the meaning of algorithm, as in the term algorithmic language. But to include the work with the numbers itself has a striking parallel to the inclusion of subroutines for some arithmetic operation in an algorithmic program. By combining the original meaning with our modern meaning, algorithm is "a play with symbols according to rules". In particular, the general concept falls into the line of Leibniz, who in his *Lingua characteristica universalis* and in his *Calculus philosophicus* had originated the idea to express concepts through symbols and to manipulate them by working on the symbols – an idea that has found its breakthrough in modern symbolic logic and formal languages.

The dual number system

Leibniz, however, is usually mentioned in connection with his advocating the base two radix system (*arithmetica dyadica,* 1703). Compared with the invention of the radix system this was a relatively minor step. Moreover, the use of a base two radix system is evident in the multiplication technique which is illustrated by the example

25 × 43	
25	43
12	~~86~~
6	~~172~~
3	344
1	688
	1075

which can be dated back to ancient Egypt.

The calculating engines

Radix notation and the use of the decimal carry characterize the calculating machines that followed Pascals design. Leibniz spent 24 000 Taler without achieving full success, and in the 18th century the German pastor Philipp Matthäus Hahn is to be mentioned for his instruments of high handicraft culture. With the beginning of the 19th century, industrial manufacturing enters the picture. Gauss could already have bought such a machine – but evidently he did not use a desk calculator.

In the early machines, multiplication and division was only done half-automatically. But even the mechanization of the four species was not enough. For the interpolation with fixed differences, a routine algorithm had to be repeated on and on. For the calculation of tables, mechanization of this process promised remarkable facilitation. Charles Babbage, who starts 1823 – a century too early – building the Difference Engine, fails and is called a fool for designing the Analytical Engine, but Konrad Zuse, George Stibitz and Howard Aiken put the idea into work. At the eve of the Second World War, the immediate tasks are ballistic tables and similar problems. And soon the new instruments become more powerful.

The renaissance of Numerical Analysis

The development that takes place after the first electronic computers, ENIAC in USA, EDSAC in Great Britain and many others produces quite soon devices that allow to do everything in scientific computation. The dream of the numerical analyst is fulfilled: a machine performs, fully automatically, his computations, his cumbersome and lengthy computations, that had always been under the dread of human mistakes. Within short time, numerical analysis is in the center of interest; the numerical analyst, who had a bitter life since the times of Jacobi, being frequently despised by his colleagues who preferred to indulge in abstract geometry, analysis and algebra, feels the excitement of the new possibilities. But numerical analysis is in a desolate shape, reflecting the lack of appreciation by its contemporaries. Many methods had been developed in the hundred years since Gauss and Jacobi, but they are scattered in the literature and there is no systematic comparative theory. Many had been discovered by scientists who had a need to perform large computations, geodesists, physicists, even, in the case of factor analysis, psychologists, and who were left in the lurch by the mathematicians. A compilation by Bodewig, in 1948, of methods for the algebraic eigenvalue problem, had to appear in an obscure journal. A re-invention of methods persisted for quite a time. But numerical analysis developed rapidly into a well-organized, independent subject. The need for error-analysis brought new impulses and today we have a flourishing discipline, a respectable branch of mathematics, which from time to time even nourishes mother mathematica.

The use of computers in the realm of military and political power

During the Second World War, it became clear that the use of computers was not restricted to the construction of ballistic tables; in fact, that the computer was to become an essential instrument in the technological development of weapons. In Germany, Schreyer proposed in 1937 to use electronic tubes for computing circuits – his thesis was declared by the Government to be secret. Support for the first models of computers was given on all sides by the government, mainly by the military authorities. Two technological results of the Second World War have in particular stimulated, financed and somewhat corrupted a generation of computers: Atomic energy and missiles. It was not earlier than in 1951 that the first non-military use of a computer in the US was registered – a UNIVAC I was used by the Bureau of Census for the 1950 Census work. This UNIVAC was also the first computer that was adapted to the needs of business data processing.

The calculation of neutron diffusion in reactors and the calculation of supersonic flow around projectiles demanded, however, a rapid increase in the power of computers – an increase in speed as well as in reliability. Input and output for this type of computation is not so deadly important, and correspondingly the appropriate devices develop less rapidly. In the Soviet Union, for example, alphanumeric input and output came relatively late, but this did not prevent this country from developing the hydrogen bomb.

The impact of atomic energy is of particular importance. Neutron diffusion can be modelled directly, the corresponding Monte Carlo methods are of relatively slow convergence and hence quite time-consuming. Nevertheless, in view of the complicated boundary conditions the practical problems show, there is not much that can be done otherwise, at least at the present time.

Faster, Faster

Thus, we find the construction of monsters, the NORC (IBM, 1955), the LARC (Remington Rand, 1957) and the STRETCH (IBM). Faster, faster is the battle cry. The costs are in no reasonable relation to the effect, but, as usual in this field, "the sky is the limit". The net effect is a tremendous gain in technological knowledge, which enables the industry that could benefit from this warm rain, to be ahead of its competitors. The deplorable fact that the world market in computers is unbalanced, is partly due to this fact.

Scientific computation

But over this concern, we should not forget that through the use of computers, e.g. in the neutron diffusion problem, an enormous stimulus was fed back to numerical analysis as well as to mathematics in general. Overrelaxation and alternating direction methods, for example gave impulses to the theory of positive matrices and to graph theory and provided hitherto unsolved problems in the theory of functions of several complex variables.

We should also keep in mind that both atomic energy and missiles so far have not led to war between the great powers and have not even been used in the conflicts some of the great powers had with others during the last 25 years. A third field, which after the year 1957, when the first Sputnik appeared on the sky, was another major user of computers, the calculation of space orbits, has also brought forward only peaceful demonstration so far, although the prestige aspect of Moon and Venus flights seems to be well understood by all sides.

To continue with a list of scientific computations which are in this sense even more peaceful, would take quite a while. Let me list instead some applications where still the pressure is for Faster, Faster (and more recently, since money is getting tight, even for Cheaper, Cheaper): There are, first of all, calculations of magneto-hydrodynamics in plasma physics with the goal of a controlled fusion. While this could turn out to be not feasible, two other problems which would bring considerable benefit to mankind are still out of our reach for some orders of magnitude because of their complexity: the calculation of a world-wide several day weather forecast with high reliability and a similar forecast for tides. Furthermore, to mention an application of international importance: satellite geodesy needs extensive use of computers in order to join and fit existing geodetic networks.

Computer science

In the foregoing deliberations, computation has been understood as being restricted to numbers. Real (or complex) numbers, sometimes integers, are the results wanted from a computer. Thus, a computer handles numbers. But a computer can do more than this. Numbers are built from figures, figures are symbols and thus, the computer manipulates symbols. Not knowing what the symbols stand for, it also handles symbols with other than arithmetic meaning. Referring to an earlier statement, that algorithm has the general sense of "a play with symbols according to rules", we should expect that modern computers can do algorithms in the general sense.

Our thesis is the following: Although derived and built originally for scientific computation in the numerical sense, the computer obtained – almost by itself – the more general capability of performing algorithms.

It is this ability which we mean and study under the heading "computing science", the numerical computation being only a special case. Scientific computation was and still is the stirr-up for computing science.

To start with the first part of our thesis: most of what is to be added to a desk calculator to make it a computer does not directly depend on what arithmetic functions the desk calculator has. A desk calculator for some strange special purpose, having nothing than the operations of the harmonic mean $s = ab/(a+b)$, the arithmetic mean $s = (a+b)/2$ and squaring, would still need and deserve the same control unit, address system and storage as a conventional one in order to become a computer. To what extent the structure of an average today's computer is independent of numerical characteristics can be seen from the description of a modern up-to-date algorithmic language in a formalized semantics, for example in the ALGOL 68 Report of the IFIP WG 2.1, edited by A. van Wijngaarden and collaborators.

Thus, the EDSAC of Maurice Wilkes already could do editing, could put together text. Clearly, whether a computer has the ability of doing "any play with symbols" does not depend on the availability of other symbols than figures, since any symbol that would be needed could be coded from other symbols. But surely, the use of binary coding already for numbers, in particular the use of base two radix notation suggested to code whatever is needed somehow in binary form. Thus, every play with symbols was possible as soon as every bitwise operation was disposable. It is the historical merit of John von Neumann and his school, that modern computers are universal in this sense. Thus, von Neumann was fulfilling the Leibniz ideal.

But, as we know, von Neumann gave not only the full algorithmic power to the computer – with the unification of data and instruction storage, he opened the possibility of a computer working on its own program. Using, in a timid way, this pandora box first only for certain address calculations, progress led soon to Rutishauser's likewise ingenious idea of the program that translates a program. Thus, in 1952, before the first program for mechanical differentiation was ready, Rutishauser opened the door for the programmed program, i.e. to something which developed into selfextending algorithmic languages, into unstratified languages.

In computing science, we study now the structure of the computing process. We define algorithmic languages that exhibit structures of the computing process and allow us to express computing processes in these structures, to do "structured programming" in the sense of Dijkstra. This is the central subject, the core of computer science, all the other themes are grouped around and derived from it.

This much about comput*ing* science. But what about comput*er* science. Sometimes, there seems to be a Chinese Wall between the people using the one and the people using the other term. But the discrepancy originates only from a historical and too narrow interpretation of the word computer. A computer, in the modern sense, is a computer system, a conglomerate of hardware and software with an irrelevant interface between the two, and this computer system is the embodiment of all possible structures of the computing processes. In this sense, the difference between computer and computing disappears.

We have seen that and how scientific computation has led to computer science. Computer science, vice versa, can be expected to pay back to scientific computation by providing it with a powerful tool. Scientists, that have more recently expressed their concern about the so-called "software crisis", the danger that a cancerous development strangulates programming, should be given our assurance that computer science can master the computer.

IFIP AND THE EXPANDING WORLD OF COMPUTERS

by

E.L. HARDER

Pittsburgh

During IFIP's first ten years, its triennial congresses covered every aspect of the growing technology of information processing. However the work of the technical committees, and specialized working conferences, was restricted to a much more limited range of basic developments, urgently needed in spreading the effective use of the computer more widely in the world. These were the *Multilingual Glossaries*, the basic work on *Programming Languages*, including ALGOL, and *Computer Education*.

Only in 1967 was the Special Interest Group, *IAG*, established to serve the specific needs of the *Administrative Data Processing* community, and the fourth technical committee formed to organize the international interchange in the highly important application of *Computers in Medicine*. The fifth technical committee, for *Applications in Technology*, was established in 1970.

Now IFIP enters its second decade, as the major international professional organization, responsible for providing the scientific interchange in this field. It is particularly important that it appraise the *future of information processing* as accurately as possible, in order to direct its future program of activities most effectively. To this end there have been numerous discussions and papers. There has been a most important internal activity of the *Future Policy Committee,* which has resulted in strengthening and broadening the IFIP organization. And there is an *Activities Planning Committee,* which as part of its modus operandi, has organized this conference in Bled (Spring 1971), for presentation and discussion of various ideas on the subject.

That "Information Processing" is an "Expanding World" is now amply evident. In a little over two decades, starting from almost zero, it has become a one hundred billion dollar ($100,000,000,000) investment in manpower and equipment. Some 70,000 computers are now in use. Administrative Data Processing is now the largest single application (60%), followed in turn by scientific data processing, the computer instrument business (minicomputers), special purpose applications (in space technology, banking, air traffic, etc.), communications and computer networks, and others.

In the first decade large scale developments and applications were limited to a few countries, including particularly the United States, where very large investments were made in both hardware developments and applications. However scientists throughout the world were contributing greatly in ideas and thoughtful background developments. This is evidenced in the early UNESCO Congress of 1959, as an aftermath of which IFIP was born. In the next decade the computer world was greatly broadened. For example between 1960 and 1965, while the investment in computers in the United States was increasing 5 to 1, that in the rest of the world was increasing 70 to 1, reaching by 1965 some 38% of the investment in the United States. Since 1965 this trend has been continuing.

Appraising the future

There are, of course, several ways to appraise the future of information processing. It may be approached from the basic idea of *artificial intelligence.* What can a computer do (with suitable programs), and what must always be done by man's imagination and mental facility? How much of mental work can be duplicated by "artificial intelligence"? This gives some concept of the extent to which computers may eventually be used in the world, although it avoids the sticky problem of economics, manpower, and time-scale, in which this might be achieved. It does, however, give very valuable insight into the potentialities, and guidance to the more long range developments in which IFIP is concerned. IFIP is currently studying how best to organize its work on artificial intelligence, for it is expected that this activity will spawn many of IFIP's exploratory ventures into the unknown future of information processing.

Another approach is based on the extrapolation of past trends and extension of developments already in use in parts of the world, to the less developed countries. Here IFIP has a most important role and is continually increasing its effectiveness.

A third approach is simply for the knowledgeable people, within the IFIP family, to sense particularly important future developmental or application areas of information processing, in which IFIP, as an international organization, can be particularly effective. It is through proposals of this kind that almost the entire present IFIP program has been formulated. As the knowledge of IFIP extends more deeply into the member country organizations it can be expected that such proposals will expand, and that the work of the IFIP Future Activities Committee, and General Assembly will be primarily that of determining the best use of IFIP resources among these proposals.

Still a fourth approach, and that which is explored in this paper, is a consideration of the barriers which now impede the progress of information processing, and a study of the developments which are under way, or proposed, and their effectiveness in overcoming these barriers. In the early and midfifties, when good, 'first-generation' computers were first becoming available, highly spectacular results could often be achieved with this new tool, never before available. Particularly in the scientific area, the pay-off was manyfold, and almost immediate. However, with maturity, most of these easily-met needs were filled, and further progress hinged on solid technological developments, which broke down some of the existing barriers.

What then are these barriers that are impeding the extension of information processing in all the diverse areas?

1. *Geographic.* First there is the geographic barrier, already mentioned. Effective use of the new tool has been limited to areas in which capital resources, and trained technical manpower, were available, and in which the state of the economic and scientific development was such that the full power of the computer could be utilized. A "critical mass" of necessary calculations was soon reached, that required large scale computers, which alone afforded low unit cost of calculation. This geographic barrier is now being rapidly demolished by a number of developments which will be mentioned.

2. *Economics.* A second barrier is economics. It simply costs too much with present technology. The cost barrier may be in the computer itself, in the preparation of the data, or in the programming, or in a combination of all three.

3. *Problem complexity.* Some problems are simply too complex, at present, to reduce to the exact formulation required for the computer to be of real help. Many of the problems of optimizing the use of the resources of the world fall in this class.

4. *Man-machine problem.* Perhaps it is the man-machine problem, which is the difficulty. Adequate communication

has not yet been worked out between the man and the machine. One has only to make an airline reservation, or a banking transaction, to realize the vast amount of work, and investment, that has now made it possible for relatively untrained clerks, with no knowledge whatever of the computer, to utilize effectively the great power of this machine, – in the few areas where this barrier has already been breached.

5. *Sensors not available.* Perhaps the sensors are not available to measure the quantities on which the calculation must be based. In 1971 there exists no practical sensor for measuring, on-line, the thickness of chrome being deposited on a strip of steel, moving over a mile a minute, in order to use a process control computer.

6. *The people who understand the problem don't understand the computer.* Perhaps the people who understand the problem do not understand the computer. This, at one time, characterized practically all applications that have now been successfully made. The developments which breach this barrier will be mentioned.

7. *Distances too great.* Perhaps the distances are too great for the data transmission. The correlation between the developments in data transmission and the solution of computer network problems is remarkable.

8. *Takes too long.* Perhaps it just takes too long. Answers, however poor, must become available sooner. The decisions in business, industry, and government must go on, day by day. Identification of the developments which are breaching this barrier provides a remarkable correlation with the progress in the use of computers in operational areas.

9. *Too big.* Perhaps the computer is too big to put into the space vehicle, or into your vest pocket. Even with integrated

circuits, the computer has a very long way to go to equal the overall processing density of the brain and its associated sensors. Each step along the way will open up extensive new application areas.

The capability of a present-day minicomputer, with more power than a first-generation (Vacuum-tube) computer requiring 70 tons of airconditioning capacity to keep it cool, sets forth dramatically the influence of size (and cost) reduction, through the very impressive list of new applications that it has made economic, and practical.

Incentives

All nine of these barriers act to varying extents in the different application fields of computers. However, lest I overstress the problems, I hasten to cite the tremendous incentives which will most certainly assure their ultimate solution.

The scope of application of information processing is as broad as information itself, although to date effective computer applications have been made only in limited areas. For example, if we consider the three elements fundamental to all human activities indicated in fig. 1 – information, energy, and materials – all of these are required for the physical things we need, i.e. housing, food, transportation, and communication. However, information plays the distinct role that it is also the substance of all of our mental activities, i.e. education, literature, government, law, and the accumulated knowledge of the world. Thus the field of information processing extends far more broadly than either energy or materials, and can eventually become more important, as our needs for energy and materials become adequately met.

There is another measure, already very apparent in the highly developed countries, which will surely follow as the state of development increases in other parts of the world. In the United States, for example, the labor force has recently passed over the boundary from more than half production workers to more than half service workers, who, as you realize, deal more with information, and less with materials and energy. Actually, it required less than 30 years for the work force in the United States to change from over 50% farmers to the present level of less than 10%, required to produce all of the food. It is predicted that in even a shorter length of time, less than 10% of the labor force will be required for all of the production work, with the service activity accounting for 90%.

This stresses even further the increasing importance of information and its processing in the economy of the world, and makes us aware of the formidable forces almost certain to be applied in breaching the barriers which have just been cited.

Background

In order to discuss the current and proposed future developments, and their impact in pushing back the nine barriers

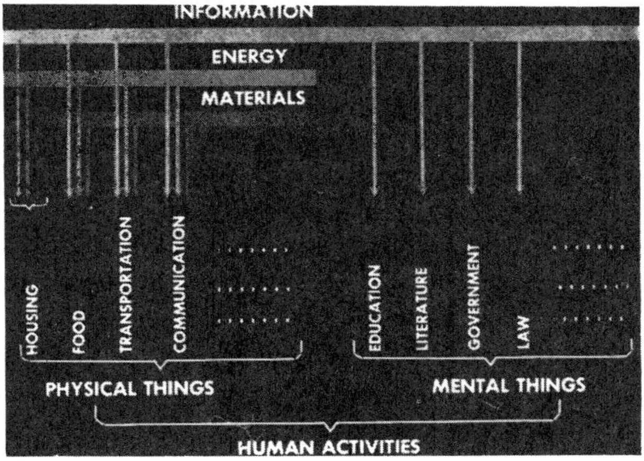

Fig. 1. Information involvement in human activities

which have been cited, it is necessary to give a very brief background. I shall necessarily use illustrations from the field of engineering and manufacturing, in which my experience has centered for over four decades. The reader will readily find parallels in his own field of activity.

Since 1950 as one barrier after another has been pushed back, there has been paralleling progress in many different areas of computer application. From the very first, perceptive managers have considered the possibility that once a salesman had entered an order, the product could be delivered, with all the intermediate steps being automated, at least as far as the information flow was concerned. However, the first application of the digital computer, back in 1950 to 1955, was to the more complex mathematical problems arising in design engineering – calculation of the vibration modes in blades, stresses in steam piping, solution of the electrical network – problems that were very difficult or impossible to solve without a computer. Nuclear diffusion, and the transient torques in shafts and couplings are other examples.

Complete designs

By 1958 complete designs were being made for a number of products. Many well known products, such as electric ranges, and refrigerators, are mass produced, and are designed only once every few years. In these cases optimizing is of course extremely important, but a combination of manual and computer techniques can be used, since it is done only once every few years.

There is however another category of products in which every order must be designed. Such products include large motors, generators, power transformers, heat exchangers, and small turbines. For these products the variability is so high as to preclude predesigning, and it is in this area that complete design by computer is most important, so that it can be made an in-line automated process. Such programs have been in use since 1958 for induction motors and power transformers, and there are continual efforts in extending the area where this is possible.

Large equipment and systems

Finally in very large equipment – large turbine-generators, large power transformers, and large systems, both the variability and complexity are so great that there is almost no possibility of ever programming the complete design. The computer plays an important role in many parts of the design, however. Improved methods of simulation, optimizing techniques, scheduling algorithms, and methods of dealing with stochastic variables, are the important developments that are pushing back the limits of our ability to deal with very large systems.

Order service and manufacturing information

Quite well along by 1960 was the extension of automatic information processing to the order-service function, and to operations that had required drafting, preparation of manufacturing information, and the scheduling of production. Production control, which is easiest for mass produced items, becomes increasingly complex for the individually designed items, and so complex for the large machines and systems that its fulfilment is still many years off. Such extremely complex man-machine interplays depend not only on the improvement in hardware and programming, but on the experience and knowledge gained in one generation of experience and techniques, in order to make possible the next step, with an order of magnitude improvement. It is at least five years per step, often ten.

Mass data processing

Paralleling the flow of information along with a particular order are the mass data processing programs of the plant, – payroll, materials control, manufacturing information, production control, and accounting. Each order going through draws information from all of these, and in turn contributes its component of information to them.

Warehousing and telecomputing

For the mass produced products, distributed through warehouses, the managers' dream of computer use was realized much sooner. The complete transaction, from order entry to shipment and billing, is typically handled by a computer, which stores the inventory, and programs, and a network of communication lines to several hundred sales points, and to the warehouses and plants involved. As the size and quality of mass memories increased, and the required technology was developed, regional batch systems of 1958 grew to national, on-line telecomputing systems of distribution by 1964.

Controlling the tools

Even in the earliest concept of the automated factory, there was a computer, which, after having produced the design, and the manufacturing information, could actually run the machines that produced the product. To examine the progress in this direction, we must divide manufacturing into fabrication, such as I have been describing in the electrical manufacturing industry, and processing, such as may occur in steel, paper, rubber, and oil, where an essentially continuous process is involved. The process-control computer, while old in concept, has become one of the most interesting current developments. Although it is hampered by the lack of sensors, of adequate mathematical models, and of sufficient knowledge to organize the procedure for computer handling, the process-control computer is none-the-less making great progress. It is being extended to many areas that one might not ordinarily think of as a process, simply controlling instrumentation systems for all sorts of things (patient monitoring in hospitals, street traffic-light control).

The most nearly paralleling development in the fabrication industries is the use of numerically-controlled machine tools, where much of the design information can be imparted to a tape control for discontinuous processes of machining, drilling, boring, milling, contouring, etc. This is an extremely interesting case of solid developments pushing back barriers, which will be developed later.

Programming developments

What progress has been made in programming? To what extent has this eliminated the barriers? What of the future? Unfortunately, compared with the hardware developments, programming, for all its brilliant achievements, has been fighting a losing battle. At least for engineering and manufacturing, the cost, which was equally divided between hardware and programming 10 to 15 years ago, is now one third hardware and two thirds programming. In spite of the fantastic improvements that have been made in programs that can be generated per dollar, or per hour, the cost reductions in the hardware have been still greater, and this places the present burden of progress squarely in the programmer's lap. I use the term "programming" broadly here, meaning the entire effort that must be made to adapt the operation to the computer, – concept, analysis, programming, everything.

Let us first trace the progress that has been made. In 1954 the computer stood virtually alone; the programmers had to make the binary to decimal conversions and call for operations in the machine code. It is almost impossible to conceive what this means, unless you have been through it. Naturally the progress was extremely slow.

Then came the symbolic assembly program in 1956, compilers, such as FORTRAN, in 1958, and operating systems in 1960. With the realization of all these aids, the prediction was that the next programming contrivance would eliminate the rest of the work, and thereafter the programmer could live a life of ease; the only questions – what new developments? – what was this new contrivance to be?

1971: New developments – problem-oriented languages, minicomputers, time-sharing, on-line, displays, computer utility

Now, several years later we know the answers to these questions. Problem-oriented languages have emerged as one of the most powerful developments for pushing back the barriers in each individual field. Several examples will be given. Also notable on the list of developments is the minicomputer, which has to a considerable measure divorced low unit cost of calculation from extremely large size. Almost equally important are time-sharing, the on-line computer, displays, and one of the most powerful uses of time-sharing, – the extension of computer capabilities through communication circuits to individual user consoles, – as well as the development of this concept into the future in the form of the computer utility.

These developments are frontal attacks on some of the main barriers that have prevented further extension and advancement of computing into a great many areas. They are not easy developments; none of them is. But they are the kind of solid developments upon which the future of information processing rests.

Following are examples of the problem-oriented languages. One was the early DYANA program for point mechanics; for dealing directly with masses, springs and levers; for determining the natural frequencies or the time-solutions, without ever leaving the terminology native to that field. It has been highly developed and expanded in later versions by different scientific groups. Typical problem-oriented languages for machine-tool control are APT and CAMP-II, which is so efficient in a language native to machine tool operations, that a paper-tape program over a mile long, for machining a turbine-generator frame, can be economically produced, even when it is used only once. And there is the COGO language of civil engineering for highway design.

The steam heat-balance program in engineering makes it possible to express the system to the computer, in terms of turbines, valves, boilers, and heat exchangers. The computer then organizes the mathematical problem and solves it, showing the steam conditions throughout the system.

These substantive new developments are helping to answer the economic problem "it costs too much". The problem-oriented language eliminates a lot of the programming. The time-shared computer makes it possible to rent a little bit of a big computer when you need it, and where you need it. Also it reduces the cost of normal programming, by making access to the computer easier and more frequent. It makes possible engineer-in-the-loop type design operations, such as COGO.

Problem-oriented languages

In using the term "problem-oriented language", and in stressing the importance of this development in pushing back the barriers to automatic data processing, I want to make it clear that the concept here involves much more than simply expressing things in a familiar language. An expert element is introduced, which increases the capability markedly, in addition to being able to present the original problem in a familiar way. For example, in the steam heat-balance program cited the entire technology for solving the heat-balance problem is built into the program. In the COGO program for highway design, all of the technolo‹ › for calculation of cuts, fills, and curves, is built in. And in the MIDAS program – DAS means digital-analog-simulation – and MIDAS means modified-integration, digital-analog-simulation, not only is the digital computer able to accept the information about the forcing functions and equations in terms native to the dynamic problems handled in this way, but it also has full instructions as to how to deal with this class of problem, given this input. The fact that the language is "problem-oriented" makes this possible. Now we are dealing with one class of problems, and can therefore go a great deal further in being specific about what is to be done.

This is a common characteristic of all of the problem-oriented languages with which I am familiar, – the APT program, the DYANA program, etc. Their power in the extension of computing lies in the fact that the expert knowledge, of skilled analysts in particular fields can be incorporated into the programs, together with a language which is native to the field, or nearly so. They can thereby break down the barriers of economics, of lack of familiarity with the computer, and of time.

This is the road of progress – not an easy one to be sure – but a road of widespread applicability. One can think of almost no field to which automatic information processing is applicable, where this method of attack cannot be used, – in biomedical, in art, in language translation, in information retrieval, and in simulation of different kinds.

Problem-oriented-languages provide a new medium for transporting skills from group to group, or from one part of the world to another, and for combining skills of different kinds. The programs for machine-tool control have successively benefited from skills in mathematics (particularly geometry), and programming skills available in the original development environment (MIT), from detailed knowledge of the economics and optimizing needed in the fabrication industry (Westinghouse – CAMP), and from the excellent theoretical and practical knowledge of machine-shop technology available to the EXAPT group in Germany. All of these skills are now available in many of these languages for use all over the world. People who "don't know the computer", but who understand their manufacturing problems, can now use the computer through these problem-oriented languages. Material progress is made in pushing back the following barriers; geographic, economic, complexity, man-machine problem, lack of understanding of the computer, and time.

Time-sharing systems

Time-sharing systems have developed so rapidly that they are now in use in all major computer centers of the world, both on large scale and minicomputers. Again, the barriers lowered are those of economics. It often costs less to program if one can have the computer help in little pieces. Large problems do not have to be completely programmed. The engineer can be in the loop. He can rent a little bit of a large computer. If the problem is too complex, decisions do not have to be all preplanned. The complex problem is broken down into a series of small simple problems. In the man-machine interface great flexibility is provided. The communication problem, to all intents and purposes, is solved. A designer in a small plant in a remote facility can have the same direct access to a powerful computer as his counterpart in the metropolitan center. Access time, a big bugaboo of the past, is cut by several orders of magnitude. A single system can carry an extremely flexible compiler, for the most sophisticated user, requiring 1000 or 2000 pages of instructions to describe it. The same system may carry a simple, but very powerful interpreter, for the occasional user, requiring only one or two pages of instructions.

Cost per calculation

One measure of the progress in computer hardware is the continually reducing unit cost of calculation. Hardware cost continues to be important, even though analysis and programming now frequently constitute the largest part of the cost. This is, of course an overgeneralization, in that, for practically all large simulation jobs, and for the majority of all direct production work, that goes on year after year, once programmed, the hardware cost itself is a vital economic factor. This covers almost the whole field of public and private administrative data processing, the largest computer application, throughout the world.

In fig. 2, I use a measure adopted many years ago, a com-

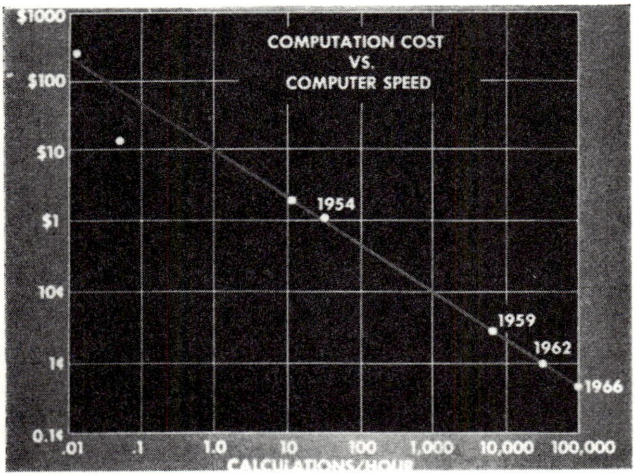

Fig. 2. Progress in reduction of computing cost with time, and size, and speed of computer

putation requiring two weeks on desk calculators by two engineers, at a cost of $300. That gives some idea of how long ago it was. This calculation can be done today for about 0.3 cents on a very large high-powered computer. The chart therefore mixes up two factors, – increasing size of computer, and increasing capability with time. Rough rules-of-thumb for these that have worked out well in planning for many years, are the following. For the same amount of money one should get twice as much computing every three years. With a larger computer, at a given time, for twice the amount of money one should get four times as much computing. When these two factors are combined there results the comparison from the tiny desk calculator of 1929, to the giant machine of today, at a gain of 100,000 to 1.

For the large simulation, for example simulating the detailed action within a nuclear reactor, it is this combined factor that counts. Reduced unit cost on the largest computer available opens up extensive new areas where simulation is feasible. The limits in this direction are a long, long way off. All the computer tapes in the world could not store the positions of the molecules in one cubic centimeter of gas, missing by a factor of about ten to the fifth power. So with any practical computer one can imagine the degree of approximation involved in representing the detailed nuclear activity within a reactor, or in the long range prediction of the weather.

Data communication

There are two important developments that I would like to mention in closing. One of these is the *cost of data communication.* In the early days, in systems work, we could provide a phone line, or rent a corresponding circuit, for $4 a mile a month. Now, as we deal with large systems and we get into Telpac C, and Telpac D, the incremental rental cost, in this area works out to be 10 cents a mile a month, a reduction of 40 to 1 from the previous figure. For a telegraph grade circuit it would be one cent per mile per month, not counting the terminal equipment, or a 400 to 1 reduction.

This completely changes the thinking and economics, as regards national systems. In this incremental range a voice circuit across the United States for $300 a month becomes negligible compared with other computer costs, to the point where a plant in California can economically use a computer in New York. Thus all kinds of networks in the private domaine are becoming national in scope. With the new communication facilities that are opening up via satellites they may well become world-wide in the future.

Education

The other matter is that of *education*. The AFIPS Survey of 1966 showed a strong correlation between the use of computers in educational institutions and the progress in the use of computers in that area. This emphasis on computer use and education in computers, is leading the new generation to turn to computers whenever there is information to process, just as the old generation turned to machines when there was physical work to be done. A typical large university computer center has some work going on, at least graduate work, from every department in the university, and in some cases with not over 10% from any one department.

With the increased use of computers, governments and universities are increasing the stress on computer education all over the world. I have mentioned the bottle-neck where the "person who understands the problem doesn't understand the computer". While it will take time, this bottleneck is being surely and steadily removed by increased computer education in schools, as well as by experience in public and private enterprises of all kinds. IFIP, through its Technical

Committee on Education and its Administrative Data Processing Group is playing a leading role, having conducted the first World Conference on Computer Education in 1970. It has developed and conducted Seminars for the training of teachers in administrative data processing, particularly for the less-developed areas of the world, and has recently prepared a guide for teaching of computers in secondary schools.

Summary

The application of computers at any time is limited by many barriers. These barriers are being rapidly pushed back by solid, enumerable developments. We can quite readily see the relationship between these developments and the future expectancy. In many of these developments, IFIP, in its international role, can be particularly effective.

We are all aware of the population explosion and the problems and pressures it generates throughout the world. It took 1600 years from the time of Christ to the year 1600 for the population of the world to double, whereas now it doubles every 42 years. The computer is the most important tool for governments and scientists to use to study the resulting problems, and to develop viable solutions.

SOME PHILOSOPHICAL ASPECTS OF INFORMATION PROCESSING

by

H. ZEMANEK
Vienna

Introduction

There are still people who think that Galilei put an end to the idea that man and earth are the center of the universe. Their argument is that we are but a grain of sand in an unimportant spot in space, in no way distinguished from other spots; that man represents only a stage in a long course of development, a super-animal after generations of animals, which, after several generations of man, will evolve towards a kind of super-man.

I think that the computer offers many arguments against this view and that information processing will convince us better than anything else that man and earth are still the center of the universe – not only because our planet represents an objective maximum of information per volume, but also because a radiation of thoughts initiated by the existence and by the use of computers will influence the philosophy and the general human thinking of the decades to come.

There will be a reconsideration of the relationship between the individual and the objective world. The view of total objectivation, which has removed man from the center of the universe, overlooks that what man feels has the greatest importance to him – most facts lose their weight with the square of distance. Integrated over mankind, this subjective judgment results in an objective fact: it is from earth that we observe space and atom, and the human body is the scaling unit for any observation, because the human sensory organs are the final receivers in any observation machinery. Denying that we are the center of the universe is not scientific objectivity and modesty; it is a misunderstanding of the information processing aspect in our activities. The intention of this paper is to show that *information processing* develops into a bridge – and into a gap – between objective and subjective domains, and to show how much support and advancement *information processing* can receive out of philosophy. Some of the loop-holes into which our art is trapped from time to time could be avoided by a proper look into the thoughts of philosophy – those of the last decades in particular.

The selection of thoughts and philosophies as well as the interpretation of their work in this paper will be highly personal and optional. The reader is invited to object and to refute, to be extremely critical. My intention is not to convince everybody of the content of the paper but to attract attention to the general idea.

This said, I can proceed to make an extraordinarily presumtuous statement:

> *The invention of the computer is the culminating point of technical development – the most important invention ever made. The computer has and will have paramount influence on the immediate and on the remote future of man.*

Surely this sounds like the usual exaggeration of the biased specialist who is unable to see the importance of even the neighbouring fields. But a comparison of man's activities with the scientific and technical achievements without and with the computer indicates that the parallel to the activity of the brain had been left open until the computer appeared. It is in this context that the information processing automaton does deserve the term *electronic brain*: it will become the central information and switching unit for most technical structures (fig. 1).

The brain is the coordinating and thinking device which makes the human body a whole; and the computer can coordinate scientific ideas and technological devices. It adds information procedures to the mass and energy procedures handled by classical machinery. Technical structures can be organized by the information processing automaton into closed systems. What more can technology achieve?

After more than twenty years of computer development, we know that such a coordination has become more than a

MAN			
Thinking Computing	Hearing Speaking	Reading Writing	Physical Working
SCIENCE AND TECHNOLOGY WITHOUT COMPUTER			
	Telecomm- munications Measurement Microphone Loudspeaker Camera Projector Screen	Printing Recording Paper, Book Journal Film, Tape	Industrial Production Automation Instrumentation Feedback-Control
SCIENCE AND TECHNOLOGY WITH COMPUTER			
ALL THE ENTITIES ABOVE PLUS			
Central Processor	Source Sink	Memory	Process Control

Fig. 1. Man versus science and technology without and with computer

dream: today, information processing embraces the piece-work of the earlier technological processes and a number of very general systems are already running under computer supervision.

Of course, the computer is *not* a brain. The wheel is not a leg, the dredger not a hand, the loudspeaker is not a mouth – why should the computer be a brain? Technical solutions are always stronger than the natural prototype, but less general; they amplify a particular faculty. Furthermore, pure thinking, thinking along strict rules like logical derivation, is a luxury activity in the first part of historical development; regulating and compensating intervention even today is the first task of the brain (not only primitive people like to be deviated from pure thinking work by a good meal or by a nice girl). Logical thinking, however, becomes a need from a certain point of sophistication onwards.

The computer is neither a brain nor a complete idiot, as one sometimes can hear. I prefer another comparison. Somebody has classified people into three categories: into the uneducated, who see only disorder; into the half-educated, who see and follow the rules; and into the educated, who see and appreciate the exceptions. The computer clearly belongs to the category of half-educated. Following rules, quickly and precisely, is the faculty in which the computer beats the human being. Another property of the half-educated, being hostile to exceptions, is characteristic to the computer atmosphere and there is the danger that this may be amplified. A strong tool tends to strengthen mediocrity. I fear that evidence in support of this statement is increasing.

It is not the mathematical power which makes the computer a device for intellectual coordination, although the numerical power alone would already be sufficient to make its invention revolutionary. It is the general symbol-handling capacity which distinguishes the computer from any prior invention. There is no intellectual activity without symbol processing, beginning with thinking, speaking and writing. In comparison with the computer, book-printing is only a copying tool – a tool, however, which multiplied the speed of information dissemination considerably and which enabled everybody to possess a private information store, called library, and an inexpensive personal news source, available at any moment of time during the day, called newspaper. The social and spiritual consequences of Gutenberg's invention were truly gigantic. The computer performs much more; it can control information dissemination at the speed of light and by all kinds of modern telecommunication; its memories will soon surpass those of the libraries; public computer networks and private consoles will soon surpass the social impact of books and newspapers – there is no risk in predicting immense psychological and spiritual consequences. And in contradistinction to book-printing, which can only duplicate information, the computer can be used for information selection and reduction; it could even be defined as an effective destruction tool for irrelevant information, if the programs would always work in this sense. (It is true, however, that unlike the book you cannot take the smallest console to bed, and there are many more advantages of the conventional media which the computer might never have.)

The computer is not only an inactive source of information like the book; it is an active control device. Computer control and integration of different technological processes yield generalized automation – a kind of extended human body with all its handicrafts, but amplified in power, speed, precision and reliability – to the limit of the current state of technological know-how. It looks as if we were making the human being unnecessary, either removing him from history or giving him a zero-hour working-week (which would be the same anyhow). This paper ought to show why this will not be true.

There is no intellectual activity without symbol processing, and from the genetic code it follows that there is no life without symbol processing. The subject is as general as a subject can be.

1. The computer

A symbol storage and replacement automaton

The computer is much more than a calculating machine, because what the electronics engineer constructed for the mathematician turned out to be a general symbol replacement and symbol storage machine in one.

A calculation in the human brain is not the creative thinking process which many people assume it to be. Most of it is entrusting to automatic symbol replacement rules learned in elementary school. When we see 6 × 7, we do not think. We cannot even afford to start a thinking process, because we would fall into one failure of the automatic process after the other. We fully automatically produce the output 42 or rather *2 carry 4.* Once you have realized this, you will discover how much of what we usually classify as active thinking in fact is automatic symbol replacement, the rules of which we have learned before, and that it is not necessarily supported by an active thinking process. General thinking lies between creative action and automatic processing. Creative thinking occurs much less frequently than we flatter ourself to be the case.

There are many replacement rules, not only in arithmetic and algebra

$$6 \times 7 = 42$$
$$6 \times 7 = 2, \text{ carry } 4$$
$$(a+b)^2 = a^2 + 2ab + b^2$$
$$Dx^n = n \cdot x^{n-1}$$

they are almost everywhere

H_2O = water
NYC = New York City
IFIP = International Federation for Information Processing
10017 = Post Office RCA Building NYC (ZIP Code)

While the given examples are only simple rules, there are also very complicated ones in any formal system (and sometimes even in only partially formal systems). They are to be found where a structure or a process can be expressed in rules – in recipies, in instruction manuals, in laws and bylaws – and all of them are virtually computer programs. Scientific calculations and book-keeping procedures posed relatively small problems when they were formulated as computer programs because they had been handled as symbol replacement mechanisms already before the invention of the computer. We are finding out presently how to treat other fields and problem classes by similar mechanisms. It seems to take a certain time to get some of the problems under control. We are, however, more than simply hopeful: we trust in the universality we know we have in our instrument.

The basis of the particular kind of universality available in the computer is its logical structure, and the mathematicians and electrical engineers who constructed the first computers certainly did not realize what basic and universal device they were creating (maybe J. von Neumann did, but he did not realize the importance of programming languages). It was only in the 19th century that mathematics took an active interest in its logical foundations. G. Boole [1] aimed at projecting logics on mathematics. It was G. Frege [2] and later authors who analyzed mathematics logically. The computer builders, however, put their device – for technical rather than philosophical reasons – from the very beginning on the basic logical functions like *negation, conjunction, disjunction* and *unit time delay*. All logics and mathematics is, therefore, built on the same grounds as the hardware of the computer, and so is all programming. A. Koestler once called the scientists sleep-walkers [3] – and one is reminded indeed of this picture when considering how the computer came into existence and how it became so universal.

From the outside, it does not matter in which code and in which technology the symbol replacement takes place. That binary coding and electronic technology are best suited is an engineering aspect and irrelevant for philosophical consideration. Even that hardware and software are mutually exchangeable to a high degree does not matter for the general investigation. Nor for the user – but it does create intrinsic manufacturing problems. Replacement of hardware by software indeed means that a product can be replaced by a form of its overhead – an equivalence of a paradoxical and frustrating nature which has not yet been duly digested by science and industry. Even the patent authorities have not yet really been able to decide how to handle this equivalence. A giant field waits for proper cultivation.

From the outside there is nothing to see around the computer but an input of chains of symbols and an output of chains of symbols. (Graphics are only translations of such chains.) On the inside, the relevant action can be described as storage of chains of symbols and as symbol replacement conform to built-in and programmed rules, again appearing as chains of symbols. Since chains of symbols can always be regarded as forming a language, the philosophical investigation of language is the right step to be taken first. Several problems of information processing which I want to touch upon must be described in language-theoretical terms before the second and real approach to the philosophy of information processing can be made.

2. Semiotics

The theory of natural and constructed languages

Philosophers have always been more or less conscious of their language as being the vehicle of thought. But it was only in the 19th century that language itself became an object of philosophical investigation. The impulse came from research into behaviour where signs play an important role. And it is from there that the insight was derived that there is no lower limit to a language: even very simple sets of signs deserve to be called *language* – the difference is one of degree and not of nature. From this it follows that the application of the word *language* in information processing is legal and appropriate.

Language theory or *semiotics* [4] distinguishes primarily three levels of investigation, called *syntactics, semantics* and *pragmatics.*

SEMIOTICS = THE THEORY OF SIGNS		
SYNTAX	RULES	CHECKING
SEMANTICS	MEANING	VERIFICATION
PRAGMATICS	USER & USE	ACCEPTANCE

Syntactics is the level of syntax, very close to the notion of grammar: the set of rules governing the relationships between the different signs. *Semantics* is the level of meaning; it describes the relationships between the signs and the objects to which they refer. And *pragmatics* is the general level of investigation, including everything else – the use of the language, the user, history and all other aspects. Since we will refer often to these levels, it pays to define them in some detail.

Syntactics

was defined by C. Morris as *dealing with the combination of signs without regard for their specific signification or their relation to the behaviour in which they occur.* The rules of combination – symbols to words, words to sentences, any kind of elements to certain patterns – in the ideal case are clear and free from exceptions. Whether a formal text, for instance, is syntactically correct or not can be checked quite easily and even automatically. Given the rules and certain selection criteria (either controlled from a higher level like meaning or just stochastical selection), formal texts can be generated by the set of rules and given formal texts can be parsed (taken apart into the syntactic elements) by automatic mechanisms.

Semantics

was defined by C. Morris as *dealing with the signification of signs in all modes of signifying.* The rules of verification – how to check whether the relationships expressed by the symbols or words are conform to those in the described world – in general are quite a problem (and we shall come back to this problem later); in the ideal case which can only be a constructed language, there might be a set of rules as to how to establish the meaning of a text. All investigation of *semantics* can aim only at an objective meaning, since its definition excludes subjective components.

Pragmatics

was defined by C. Morris as *dealing with the origin, uses and effects of signs within the behaviour in which they occur.* In natural languages, this is where any investigation has to start: find out how the users use the language and then see further, discover its grammar, for instance. For constructed languages it is inviting to start off by playing with sets of syntactic rules, but the good way again is starting from pragmatics: which functions are wanted, what goals are to be achieved. In both cases, *pragmatics* is that part of language investigation which is least suitable for systematic treatment.

It is obvious that these three definitions are hierarchical, each following definition includes the preceding one;

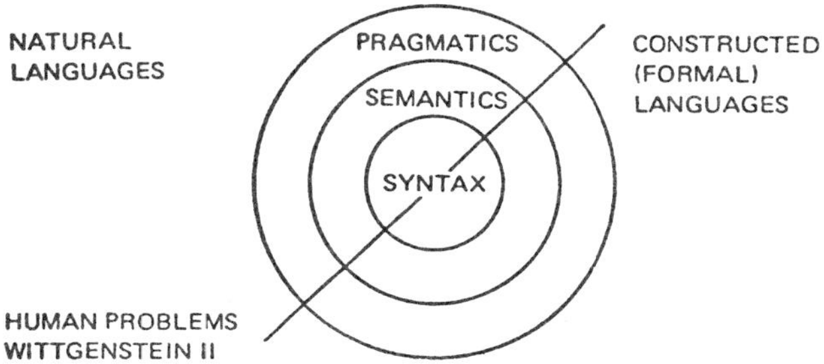

the borderlines between the three levels are not always well defined and clearly visible, but as a principle and as a thinking tool, semiotics has proved to be very convenient and efficient.

In order to make syntactics and semantics fully clear, a table shows syntactically and semantically correct and incorrect expressions of algebra where semantics is related to the volume of a cube:

	CORRECT	INCORRECT
SYNTACTICALLY	a – (b + c)	a) – bc) +
SEMANTICALLY (IN CASE OF CUBE)	$V = a^3$	$V = a^5$

Semiotics has further principles of classification. One can distinguish *natural* and *constructed* languages, description *before* and *after* generation of the described object – we will come back to these differences later.

An important other classification of semiotics has to do with the level of description. Talking about language requires a language. While natural languages are suited for any level – they are not *stratified*, as S. Gorn [5] expressed it – there can be confusion in the description if the level is not indicated. If we say that semiotics consists of nine letters, then we really mean the word *semiotics* and not the science; it is easy to see in this case that the sentence is in metalanguage which speaks about language, but still it is better to use another alphabet or to put the word into quotation marks ("semiotics"). Speaking about the metalanguage requires a meta-metalanguage, and so forth – there is no end to the sequence. The question maybe resolved one day as to whether the ultimate metalanguage will always be a natural language or whether a constructed language is possible which successfully and unambiguously will define itself.

3. Form and content

Five kinds of information

It is an elementary property of the digital computer that any processed information is coded into the same kind of sequences of bits: of binary digits or decisions – a parallel to the human body where information mainly travels in the form of pulse frequency modulation (which latter, however, is an analog form).

The same form does not imply the same content. Syntactically, already, the same sequence of a few bits may represent different symbols depending on their position, and adequate time and space frameworks are necessary for proper and correct translation. But the important difference is not on the syntactic level, it is on the semantic level. The same sequence of a few bits in the same position may have different semantic interpretations, and it is not always certain what the interpretation depends on. Conservation of meaning is the main problem of information processing when all mechanics has been brought in order. Five different classes of information shall show the difficulty (Fig. 2).

INFORMATION	SEMANTICS	EXAMPLE
NUMERICAL	SYNTACTIC	3.1415926535
PHYSICAL	DIMENSIONS	300000000 m/s
FORMATTED	DESCRIPTION	70 AUGUST 20
NATURAL TEXT	UNDERSTANDING	IN PRINCIPIO ERAT VERBUM
FORMAL TEXT	DEFINITION	IF A=B THEN GOTO BEGIN;

Fig. 2. Five kinds of information

(1) *Numerical Information*

Purely logical and numerical information is the easiest case. A string of numerals out of an alphabet corresponding to the base (2, 8, 10, 16, what ever the system is) constitutes a word in which the position of the numeral in the string establishes the interpretation. For logical and numerical information, all rules of processing are syntactically well defined, as the following lines indicate:

$$(x + y) \times z$$
$$(x \wedge y) \vee z$$
$$(x > y) \wedge (z = 1)$$
$$(\textit{is-blue}\ (x)) \wedge (\textit{is-berry}\ (x)).$$

Addition and multiplication are as unambiguous as conjunction or disjunction; the relational operators "greater" or "equal" can hardly cause doubts in the usual processing; predicate logics assumes that the decision whether a property is true or not can always be made without any doubt. Everything is projected onto bits and all kinds of clean logics handle bits and transform first into bits.

Propositional Logics

combinatorial logic:	bits → bit
relational operators:	numbers → bit

Fig. 3 (left).
Fig. 4 (bottom).

	t^{-3}	t^{-2}	t^{-1}	1	t^1	t^2
l^2	P	M,W	h	J		
l^1		F	p			
1		σ		m		
l^{-1}			η			
l^{-2}		γ				
l^{-3}				ρ		

	t^{-3}	t^{-2}	t^{-1}	1	t^1	t^2
l^3				V		
l^2				A		
l^1		a	v	l		
1		α	ω	1	t	
l^{-1}				k		
l^{-2}						

[ε] = 1, [f] = 1

	t^{-5}	t^{-4}	t^{-3}	t^{-2}	t^{-1}	1	t^1	t^2
l^5	P	M,W	h	J				
l^4		F	p					
l^3	S	σ	I	m,Q		V		
l^2		w	η,h	U		A,φ		
l^1		γ	i	a D,E	V, G	l,C		
1				α,ρ	ω,B	1	t	
l^{-1}						k	R	L
l^{-2}								μ

A area
a acceleration
B magnetic induction
C capacitance
D displacement
E electric field strength
F force
f gravitational constant
G conductance
H magnetic field strength
h Planck's constant
I electric current
i current density
J moment of inertia
k curvation
L self inductance
l length
M moment of force
m mass
P power
p momentum
Q quantity of electricity
R resistance
S Poynting vector
t time
U tension
V volume
v velocity
W work
w electromagnetic energy density

α angular acceleration
γ specific weight
ϵ dielectrical constant of vacuum
η viscosity
μ permeability
ρ density
σ surface tension
ϕ magnetic flux
ω angular velocity

	sequential logic:	streams of bits, memory
	asynchronous logic:	causes necessarily a problem
Predicate Logics		property → bit

Proper timing is a logical condition. As soon as asynchronous operation is included there may be problems, and description systems for such a logic, like the Petri network (occurrence graphs), do their best but cannot always avoid undecidable situations.

In the case of numbers, the position principle is generalized by the *comma* facility, sometimes notated by a power multiplier. Higher mathematics is a shorthand notation for a program or for replacement rules to be carried out later on numbers and based on the established rules. The construction or study of mathematical relationships independent of later application in a program is indeed more general than a final algorithmic formulation and execution, but essentailly all mathematical thinking is programming a "computor" – whether man or computer, whether the treated relationships are finally executed somewhere and somehow or not. It may be very difficult to establish the correct meaning of a mathematical notation, but in principle and by definition, any semantic problem can be reduced to the basic rules of arithmetic and logic and, therefore, it is not wrong to say that all semantics of mathematics can be reduced to syntax.

(2) *Physical Information*

Any physical quantity is understood as a product of a numerical value and a dimension or a unit; and in a well-ordered unit system, there is no essential difference between indicating the unit or the correlated dimension. Both are, furthermore, well-ordered in a time-space-framework. Dimensions are not a property of nature, by the way – they are a syntactical checking system, as their inventor, J.M. Fourier, 1822 in his *Théorie analytique de la chaleur* [6] pointed out clearly enough; which dimensions are chosen as a basic and which as derived is an arbitrary decision. Choosing the system legal now in most countries, having length, time and mass as basic dimensions and meter, second and kilogram as basic units, one gets a perfectly clear table (Fig. 3); the electric units can be treated in one more level. Putting, in another step, and again arbitrarily, the dielectric and the gravitational constants both 1 and dimensionless, it is possible to project all physical quantitities into one plane (Fig. 4).

I do not want to draw here any particular conclusion from these frameworks. What I want to show is how the physicist understands to remove semantic problems from his calculations. Once a phenomenon and its measuring problems have been cleared up, all semantic problems are taken care of by the dimensions – which fall out of any orderly physical equation. Physics is thus handled by pure mathematics, related to a logically extremely clear system of dimensions. Therefore, as long as science is physical science and proceeds like physics, there are no semantic problems in the required information processing: there is mere calculation. This explains why it was so easy to have mathematical and physical problems solved by the computer: formalization had been a tradition long before, and no semantic confusion occurred in their calculations.

(3) *Formatted Information*

Already in the computer hardware there is something which can be called formatted information; take the machine code instruction as a typical example:

DESK CALCULATOR	INSTRUCTION	NUMBER	+ 1683
MACHINE LANGUAGE	INSTRUCTION NUMBER	ADDRESS	0815 4711
ASSEMBLY LANGUAGE	INSTRUCTION CODE	NAME	ADD X3

Using formats is the method of commercial information processing too. The books of book-keeping are forms and the meaning of a field in the form or format is established beforehand and mostly outside the book. The book-keeper is a "computor": a mechanical device (even if a human being: he must stick to the rules like a machine). Book-keeping is error-free and independent of any semantic problem. And this explains why it was so easy to get commercial information and its processing into the computer. Very naturally, we are inclined to conclude that all other kinds of information processing will go equally easily into the computer. But this is a false hope.

Without knowing the semantic definitions of the fields of the format of formatted information, the meaning of the symbol chains remains more than open. Let me show you an example:

AUGUST	AUGUST	AUGUST
PRAHA	20 AUGUST 20	CSSR
PRAHA	20 AUGUST 20	CSSR
70 AUGUST 10	70 AUGUST 20	AUGUST AUGUST

This set of entries alone could not be understood. Some readers may know that the Czech author P. Kohout wrote a play with the title *August August, August* [7] where he gives a little formatting by the comma, as a hint. *August,* in Czech

FIRST NAME AUGUST	FAMILY NAME AUGUST	PROFESSION AUGUST
BIRTH PLACE PRAHA	BIRTH DATE 20 AUGUST 20	CITIZENSHIP CSSR
TOWN PRAHA	STREET 20 AUGUST 20	COUNTRY CSSR
ADMITTED 70 AUGUST 10	EMBARKED 70 AUGUST 20	SIGNATURE AUGUST AUGUST

and in German, means *clown,* and with this information, one can read the title as a first name, a family name and a profession. Extended to the police form given above, the entries absolutely require the format information or else one is completely lost. Who ever had to fill out a form for the census most probably has felt a semantic uncertainty about one or the other entry, the profession for instance, although the officers of the census who designed the format usually add on the form an explanation of the semantics they require to have attached to the fields.

I want to add another example in order to show the practical implications of the semantics of formatted information. The example comes from a practical problem of export and import statistics as handled by the typical office of statistics. There are many visible and many hidden relationships in these data which today are fed into computers where programs automatically combine the information of different statistics, making use of these relationships. But there are semantic gaps of which the programmer is not necessarily aware.

What is a *calf*? You would think you know: the young of a cow. All right; everybody understands this and it does not look like a semantic problem. With regard to parameterization, one might conclude that it is simply age that has to be considered: once all countries agree on the age at which a calf turns into a cow, the statistical problem of comparing calf statistics will be resolved. Unfortunately, this is not so. The really pertinent question is: what is *veal*? Because economy is interested in the calf mainly as the source of veal. If you now think that *veal* is the *meat of calf*, you are wrong. *Veal* is the meat of a calf that has been nourrished with milk and no grass. The parameter of age, consequently, is not sufficient for the purpose. I shall not go into more complications by discussing the *heifer* and *steer* or by asking whether indeed *every* piece of meat cut off a calf is classified as veal. The semantics of veal and calf in European or world statistics could be the subject of a doctor's thesis, and processing statistical data on calf and veal can obviously not guarantee conservation of meaning.

No syntactic checking procedure, no double precision can improve the situation. And this is typical, once the safe ground of physical science is left in information processing; processed formatted information is only as good as the definition of the semantics of the entries – and of how well this definition was respected at the input, during processing at the output and when interpreting the result.

(4) *Natural Text*

Unformatted information, a text in natural language is, of course, even more problematic. It is true that many professional languages have very much of a formal character – think of medical presciptions or of medical records. But spread over the formal expressions, there are comments with all the properties of natural language, and for natural language the semantic problem is quite open. Let me illustrate this statement by two examples.

In Goethe's *Faust* the famous professor intends to translate the bible from Latin to German. Starting with the first sentence of St. John's Gospel, he finds himself trapped in a semantic problem: he does not know how to decide between four possible translations coming into his mind for *verbum*.

Adding the entries which can be found in a German-English dictionary to the four possibilities, one is presented with a choice among more than 20 solutions:

IN PRINCIPIO ERAT VERBUM

VERBUM:

Wort	word vocable term expression
Sinn	sense intellect direction mind memory intelligence wit meaning significance
Kraft	strength power energy efficiency
Tat	deed act action achievement

It could be argued that a good translation algorithm would simply translate into the first entry, *verbum* into *word*. Indeed, this is exactly how originally *logos* was translated into *verbum*; but this translation created precisely the problem which Professor Faust cannot solve and neither can the computer. Living languages cannot be translated satisfactory: *Übersetzung ist Unfug* (Translation is mischief), said the Viennese writer K. Kraus. *Mechanical Translation* scarcely furnishes newspaper headlines in our days. One of the first to predict the unreasonableness of aiming at fully automatic high quality translation was Y. Bar-Hillel [8], and here is his famous example where the computer cannot possibly make a decision, while the human translator can:

THE BOX IS IN THE PEN.

pen, like many other words, has a double meaning and a good dictionary shows both. But what comes immediately to the human mind is the idea to associate a size relation to the problem:

pen_1 ::= writing device $<$ box

pen_2 ::= childrens cage $>$ box

Not only would a program including all possible size relations cover quite an amount of storage space – how would a program find out that size is the parameter to try out here first or early on, before searching in many other families of relationships which might be equally important in the general translation case? To dream here of parallel search at the moment is science fiction.

How powerful language and the human mind are, is shown, by the way, by a gag which Norwegian friends of Professor Y. Bar-Hillel invented for him: they constructed a big paper-made pen where instead of a cartridge it housed a pill-box. This funny object rules out the chances of proper translation of the text even for the human translator, if he does not know the circumstances.

All experience with natural language has shown that semantics is far beyond a rule-controlled system; it requires full education and escapes computer programming. We will come back to this. The computer-tailored way out of most semantic problems, followed by programming from the very beginnning, are formal languages. For there is only one way to keep semantic problems under control: to *construct* an artificial language and to remain perfectly within the domain of the construct – to use formal text instead of natural.

(5) *Formal text*

Well-known and good examples of constructed languages are *algebra* as well as *logical algebra* and, of course, *programming languages.* Constructed languages can have perfect syntax and unambiguous meaning; how to construct them properly and how to describe them adequately is, among other things, a matter of the next higher level, of the meta-language used, i.e. of formal definition of syntax and semantics. This will be discussed in the next chapter.

Summarizing the five kinds of information, it can be said

that mathematical, physical and traditional book-keeping information had been handled formally over centuries, it was known how to avoid semantic problems and how to mechanize routine processing before the computer was invented. But when the computer's possibilities of going beyond classical mechanical information processing were realized, these safe grounds had to be left and wherever this happens, one has to deal with natural texts. For such texts, in contrast to the general impression, conservation of meaning cannot be guaranteed in information processing. The failure of natural language translation, for which so much money had been spent, came as a surprise. Y. Bar-Hillel's example and his arguments were not taken seriously enough; the rules of verification do not constitute a programmable system.

Philosophy has recognized this fact but computer people are not used and not willing to accept what philosophy offers to their profession. It is the general idea of this paper to invite a change of attitude.

Before I turn to a more general description of some relevant philosophical thoughts, I want to say more about formal definition which I think is a key to many computer problems.

4. Formal definition

The precise sketch of the essential

Information processing is symbol handling, the programs are texts in some formal language, and it is necessary to describe the syntax and the semantics of programming languages with the greatest possible precision in order to make sure that the computer carries out exactly what the programmer expects and to conserve meaning. For such a language description, a meta-language is required and at this level, the question of natural or formal language appears again: should programming languages be described and defined informally or formally? From this question one can generalize to the problem of description of all information processing structures, hardware and software – is it sufficient to talk informally about them?

About this question, one more battle is going on in the long series of battles between informal and formal treatment. It is indeed not easy to see why the wonderful tool *natural language* should be abandoned. Everybody masters it and the creation of new structures can only take place in it. We shall come back to this problem later; here I want to quote only a few selected examples of conflicts between informal and formal. A battle is sure to have taken place when hieroglyphic pictures were replaced by a letter system, a typical and important step of abstraction against which a lot of arguments could be brought forward and certainly were brought forward. But the success of abstraction defeated all these arguments. A second battle happened in the middle ages when mathematics was formalized. The most successful book was written around 820 AD by the Arab mathematician Abu Dsha'far Muhammed Ibn Musa Al Khowarizmi and translated into Latin around 1200. From the title of this book the term *algebra* spread into the European languages and the term *algorithm* is derived from the birth place of the author: Khowarizm is now Khiva in the district Khorezm of the Uzbek Socialist Soviet Republic. Alkhvarizmi, as the author was called for short, was active in the move from informal to formal algebra. In his first book, he described the inheritance problems of a rich Moslem with many wives and children of different legal status mostly by examples and in natural language. In a later book, algebra is treated generally and formally, with examples from many fields, including inheritance problems.

One argument against formal algebra certainly was that the formal notation of algebra made the texts much more confusing and mystical than the complication of natural descrip-

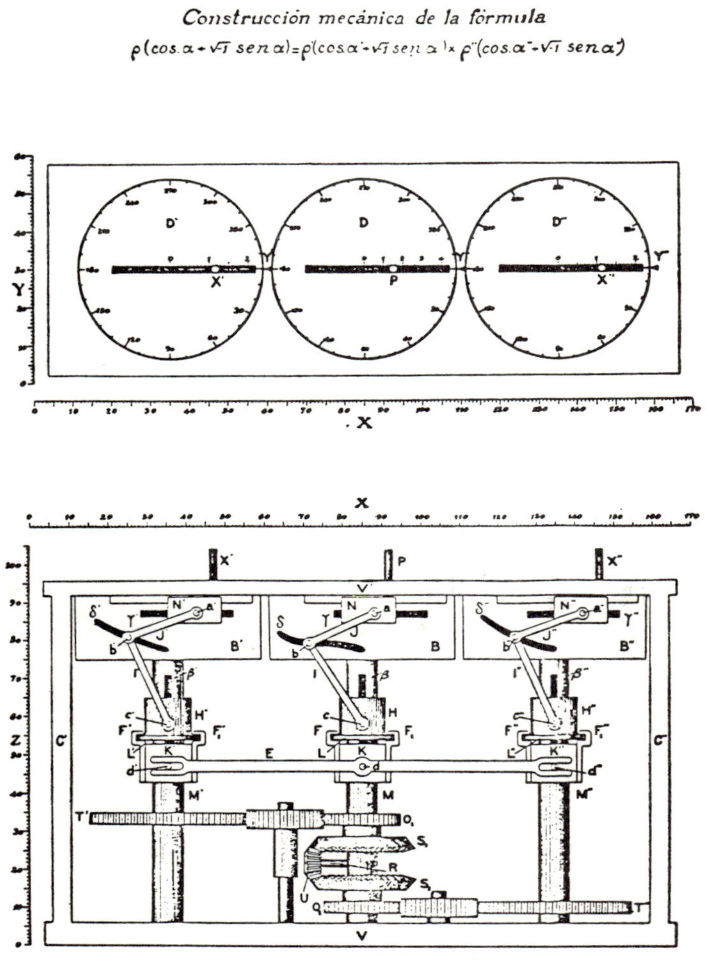

Fig. 5. Hardware defined by 31 equations (Torres y Quevedo, 1907)

·*Descripción simbólica del aparato*·

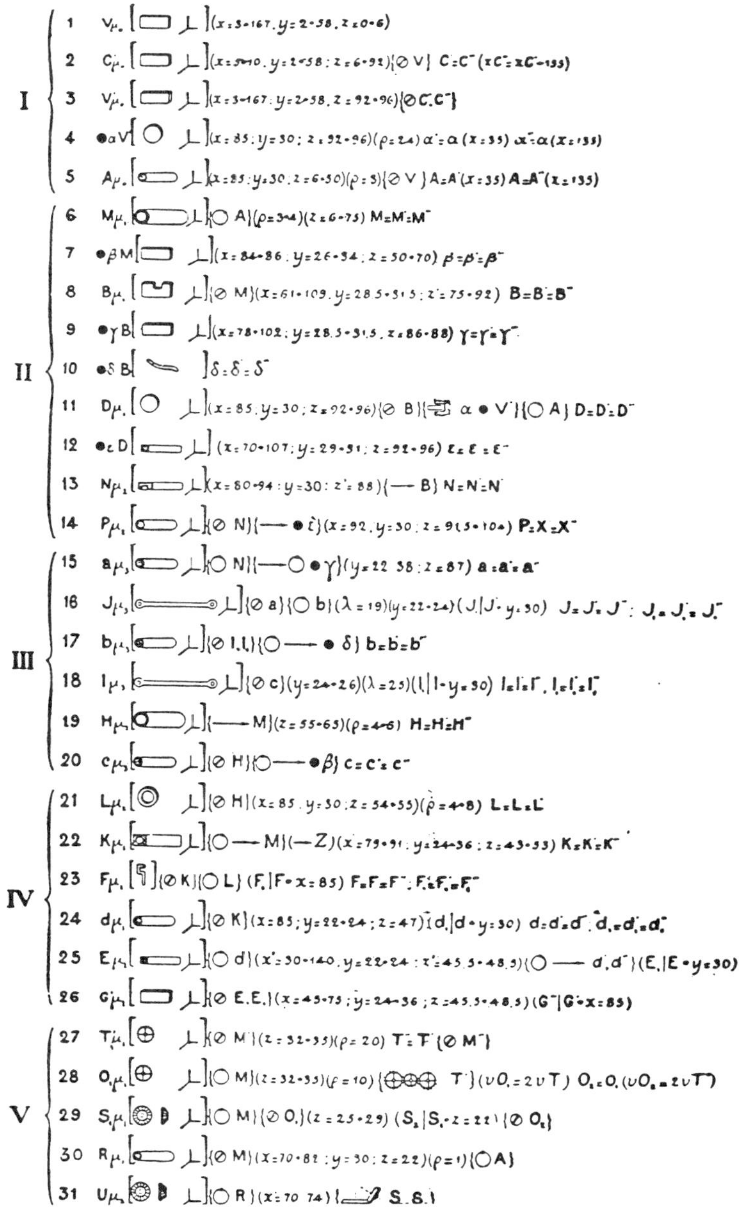

tion. Today we know that this is simply a matter of education: certainly it takes some pain to learn the formal notation, but the gain is clarity, reliability, shorter texts, more efficient thinking and general application and understanding independent of the natural mother language of the writer and reader. It is not sufficient to talk informally.

One should realize that geometry and technical drawing also have the character of formal languages. They include analog elements, but a precise treatment has to take recourse to algebra. I need not go into analytic geometry, there is an example of the early 20th century very close to information processing. The Spanish inventor of computing devices and automata L. Torres y Quevedo in 1907 proposed to a meeting of representatives of Academies of Sciences the formal definition of complicated technical drawings [9]. His example was a mechanical mathematical machine for the multiplication of complex numbers which he had published a year before. Torres y Quevedo proposed a formal description language which looks very much like a page of PROLAMAT proceedings [10] of our time, like a programming language for the control of tools by computers. In this notation, the multiplication device can be described formally in 31 lines (Fig. 5), and the box is included in the description. Torres y Quevedo's proposal was not accepted by the Academies; even scientists sometimes do not recognize the value of methodology.

Description in natural language is never precise, complete or free from contradiction. Its terms call up connotations and associations out of control of the writer. And when describing a really big structure, it is impossible to keep all features in mind at one time as it is necessary when writing about structures in natural language. The development of the computer from the calculating instrument to a universal information processing device will depend, therefore, on the speed with which formal definition technologies are introduced into the thinking, design and application of information processing – an analogon to algebraic notation for computation and to Torres y Quevedo's hardware notation, replacing and extending them.

An essential feature of formal definition technology is the economy of expression. While always speaking precisely, it must leave it to the user how much to go into details. In other words, one must be able to speak precisely even on fuzzy objects or on precise objects, the details of which are to be defined later or at another level of design; one must be able to give an exact sketch of a task to be carried out, of the essentials to be met, leaving open the free details without loss of clarity and precision. Construction by properties (by requested properties, for instance) rather than by arbitrary start elements must be possible, and semantics should be settled before syntax so that the design does not become a victim of arbitrary syntactic assumptions made before the construction of meaning – as it usually happens when design is started without formal definition methods. Formal definition is a planning and management tool.

Formal control of the syntax is the easier problem. The standard method is to construct the generation rules by which all *well-formed* sentences of the language could be produced. A complete system is called *generative grammar*; in the case of programming languages, the same principle and form of definition is known as *Backus Normal Form*

```
GRAPHIC    ::= CHARACTER | MARK
CHARACTER  ::= DIGIT | LETTER
DIGIT      ::= 0| 1| 2| 3| 4| 5| 6| 7| 8| 9
LETTER     ::= A| B| C| D| E| F| ... | Z
NUMBER     ::= DIGIT| NUMBER•DIGIT| DIGIT•NUMBER
NAME       ::= LETTER| NAME•LETTER| NAME•DIGIT
```

because the American mathematician J. Backus gave a formal definition of the syntax of ALGOL (58) by generation rules in a particular notation invented for a paper to the Paris ICIP

Congress 1959 [11]; the ALGOL group and P. Naur made full use of this method in the final ALGOL 60 Report [12].

Formal definition of semantics is rather more complicated. One can escape by reducing the enterprise to translation into a language whose meaning is considered as established. But then the problem emerges again for the other language. One possibility is the axiomatic method, but it works only in a highly elegant environment (I believe). The method I want to describe a little more in detail is related to the notion of computation – a constructive method which also works reasonably well in less elegant environments.

Its basic idea is to design a step-by-step process where each step is a well-defined transition from one set of symbols to the next set of symbols, driven by some abstract mechanism. In fact, it is even more precise to speak of an abstract machine (although such a machine is not always visible in the historic publications on the subject of computation) with well-defined transition functions leading from one state to the next. The most famous example of such an abstract machine is the Turing machine.

Generalizing the idea from computation to formal languages, one receives an abstract *language* machine, elabora-

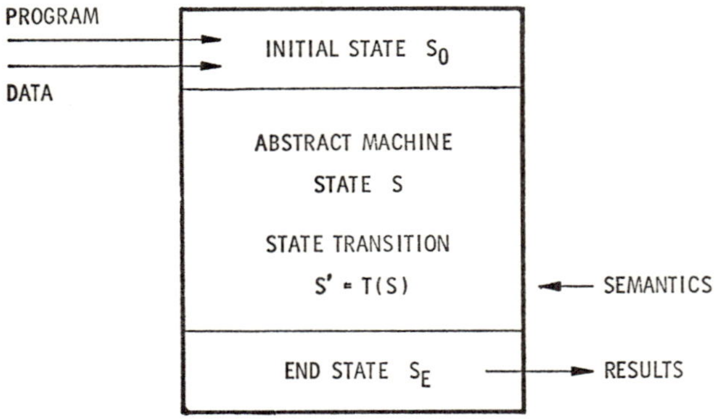

Fig. 6. The abstract PL/I machine

ting program texts in this language, PL/I for instance (Fig. 6). Starting from an initial state – which includes the text to be investigated – the abstract machine will go through a sequence of states until it reaches a final state. Looking at the sequences of states produced by a specific text, the human observer can see the meaning of the text and can perform all verifications necessary for the semantic analysis. No question remains open; when the answer is undefined, then one can definitely see that this is the case.

That such a programme can in fact be carried out even for a big programming language which had originally been informally defined, was proven for PL/I. The procedure is more complicated, because it is economical to prepare the original text before filling it into the abstract PL/I machine as such, but the final effect is as described. The documentation contains six reports of altogether more than 1200 pages – which, by the way, were printed fully automatically by a computer, i.e. by an algorithm deciding the layout including length logical formulae displaying their structure [13].

How far can the method of formal definition go? Will we be able in future not only to define formally the fields of formatted text so that every ambiguity is removed, but also to formally define the syntax and semantics of natural languages? The work of N. Chomski [14] looks rather promising for the grammar, and much effort is being put presently into the definition of semantics. In order to obtain an answer to our question, we return to philosophy, but now we will not restrict our consideration to the theory of languages – we rather will spin some threads through very general problems.

5. Philosophy

An attempt to understand the world

Philosophy is an outcome rather of doubt than of confidence. Neither the convinced belief nor the confident move within an established system will call for philosophical investigation; the motor of the latter is mistrust of what looks obvious and of what is considered as being safely established. But once the curiosity is awakened, the philosopher tries to understand the world by some principle or by some mechanism which more or less automatically will explain the universe (we do not look very much on philosophies here which are a kind of negation of this description). The philosopher, therefore, is an information processor and his attempt is similar to the one of science, but undertaken by different methods.

The relationship between science and philosophy is not an easy one. The two views of the world complement each other and neither of them really can do without the other. At the same time, careless transfer of spirit, of methods and results from one side to the other may be very bad. In fact, there is a substantial difference in the goals: science aims at solutions, while philosophy cares for questions; science is based on the common view of the scientists while what one philosopher proposes as a result is not only doubted by the others but frequently refuted. The scientist, therefore, usually looks quite suspiciously on philosophy, considers it unsafe ground. This may be allright, but one should never miss an opportunity to learn and to gain insight. Information processing is closer to the world of philosophy than any other branch of science or technology and consequently can profit most from philosophical insights. Also there will be a considerable feedback from information processing to philosophy; it may well be that the computer will help to bring forward a new period of human thought.

Early philosophy searched for a basic principle, but not so much for certainty. If certainty was hoped for, then rather from a religious belief than from a thinking effort. It was essentially in the 17th century, an offspring of the Renaissance, that the philosophical attempt started to aim at certainty and perfection (Fig. 7).

The *Rationalists* like Descartes, Leibniz and Spinoza hoped to gain clear and distinct ideas by the search of the human mind. The analysis of human thinking was expected to yield the basic elements, the irreducibles which constitute the world, so that a synthesis based on those elements will allow the construction by proper reasoning – to understanding of the world and an environment for better life. Leibniz formulated this hope in 1680 by the following words: [15]

> *Therefore, when a controversy arises, two philosophers will have no more dispute than two computerists. It will suffice for them to get writing tools and an abacus at hand, and to say to each other (in a friendly tone, if they please): Let us calculate!*

The *Empiricists* like Locke, Berkeley and Hume did not

ELEMENT	RELATION	SYSTEM	NAME
WATER	LAWS OF NATURE	ANCIENT PHILOSOPHY	THALES
ATOM			DEMOKRIT HERAKLIT
	PHYSICS	HOMME MACHINE	DE LA METTRIE
INNATE IDEA	CLASSIC LOGIC	RATIONALISM	DESCARTES LEIBNIZ
UNIT SENSATION	ASSOCIATION	EMPIRICISM	LOCKE HUME
		ASSOCIATIONISM	
	CONDITIONED REFLEX	BEHAVIOURISM	WATSON PAVLOV
PROTOCOL SENTENCE	FORMAL LOGIC	LOGICAL EMPIRICISM	WITTGENSTEIN VIENNA CIRCLE

Fig. 7. Philosophical systems

search inside the human mind; they hoped to get the irreducibles from outside, from the direct sensations. Their programme was not only close to the one of science, they indeed prepared the thinking of the scientific era, and it will be of paramount importance that contemporary philosophy has carried this attempt to the very end – to a negative end. I will try to show this in several steps.

The analysis, the empiricists say, is done by memory and by association in the human mind, which – from the outside – appears as a machine. Carried through to the extreme, this philosophy would see in certain sensory inputs the atoms from which all our knowledge is built up by the mechanism of association. While Leibniz talked about the computer as an aid for discussion, the empiricists conceived human thinking very much as information processing with input, processor, memory and output. When De La Mettrie wrote his book *L'homme machine* [16], he paid little attention to information processing structures in the body, his main interest was for the mechanical and chemical processes; too little was known about electricity and the nervous system in his time. But philosophy had, without knowing it, already much earlier given a lot of consideration to the information processing aspects of human thinking.

In particular the mechanism of *association* was a main subject of study and it is necessary to spend a few lines on it also here.

In a dictionary of philosophy and psychology [17] I found the following entry for *association*:

> *Association (of ideas) is a union, more or less complete, formed in and by the course of experience between the mental dispositions corresponding to two or more distinguishable contents of consciousness and of such nature that when one content occurs, the other content tends in some manner or degree to occur also.*

This sounds like a rather unreliable mechanism, but obviously much of the creative force of the human being is connected with it, and it looks like the product of creativity and reliability has an upper boundary above which more creativity means less reliability and vice-versa. This would have an implication for artificial intelligence and associative memories which I cannot go into here. (I did elsewhere [18], and what I found contributed to this paper.)

An early writer on the subject of association was Aristotle. In his treatise *On memory and reminiscence* he distinguishes *association by similarity, association by contrast and association by contiguity*. Locke was the first to use the expression *association of ideas* and Hume added *association by cause and effect*. Subsequently, a school of associationism was developed which tried to establish that all human knowledge is built from separate, simple and particular experiences. All knowledge, therefore, can be analysed into such experiences without remainder. The building up of knowledge happens by repetition and by association. Does this not sound like a description of the hopes of an ambitious programmer of an associative system or of an optimistic researcher in the field of artificial intelligence?

In the late 19th and early 20th century, a strong reaction against associationism arose. The basic contentions of the school were rejected and non-mechanical principles were proposed. But, at the same time, a new support for the thoughts of associationism emerged: it came from biology. The processes and the physiology of nervous associations were studied more and more. It was found that they are basic for neurobiology and that, in a certain sense, the importance of associations is much greater than the philosophers had thought so far. Pavlov in Russia stressed the use of objective methods in what he called *the study of associations* and he arrived eventually at a complete deviation of all behaviour from original (unconditioned) and conditioned reflexes. J.B. Watson in America defined psychology as the study of behaviour by objective methods and made behaviourism a general principle, a philosophy. The behaviourists reformulated the claims of associationism (as well as some new ones) in a new vocabulary; although new objections were brought forward – for instance by the Würzburg school and by Gestalt psychology – an atomistic view of mind function was dominant in the first third of our century.

So, shortly before the First World War all elements were ready for a common view of logics, mathemathics, linguistics, physics, chemistry and psychology, for a logical and atomistic philosophy. A young man recognized this situation and conceived such a philosophy – being a formal definition of the universe of nature and mind. If there is a computer philosopher, it is he, and we will be dealing with his thinking in the remainder of this paper.

6. The philosophy of perfection

Wittgenstein I and the computer

The young man was the Viennese L. Wittgenstein, born 1889 and educated as an engineer. He had very broad interests and covered many fields by his studies. What ever he did, he did with incredible intensity. He became a student of B. Russell in Oxford and of the psychologist K. Buehler in Vienna. What the *Principia Mathematica* did for logic and mathematics, what the idea of the *atom* and *quantum* did for physics and chemistry, what *associationism* intended for psychology, he generalized to an overall philosophical system. In 1921 he first published his *Tractatus Logico-Philosophicus* [19], the main sentences of which read:

1. *The world is all that is the case.*
2. *What is the case – a fact – is the existence of states of affairs.*

3. *A logical picture of facts is a thought.*
4. *A thought is a proposition with a sense.*
5. *A proposition is a truth-function of elementary propositions.*
6. *The general form of a truth-function is* $[\bar{p}, \bar{\xi}, N(\bar{\xi})]$
7. *What we cannot speak about, we must pass over in silence.*

For about 15 years, Wittgenstein was convinced that his *Tractatus* had closed the books of philosophy, as the intention of this work had been from the beginning: he had given to his treatise the title and the form of a legal *Abhandlung* – it was a trial on philosophy. A little story seems to explain best how he came by his ideas and how he understood them [20]. In a journal, Wittgenstein once saw a sketch describing the possible progress of an automobile accident. The relationships between the parts of the picture and the objects in the real world and the relationships within the two structures picture and world define exactly the state of affairs and the correct logical picture of them. Wittgenstein generalized the comparison and put it on solid logic and linguistic grounds; he defined the scientific and philosophical sentence as an element of the logical picture of the world.

The *Tractatus* is in fact a synthesis of the theory of propositional calculus and the theory of the sentence as a picture of reality. One of Wittgenstein's basic assumptions is that there are elementary sentences, atom-like statements, which he calls *elementary propositions* and which are logically and factually either *true* or *false*. A *proposition* is a logical combination of *elementary propositions*. The syntax of the well-formed picture of reality in a scientific language is, then, the set of all well-formed logical combinations of all *elementary propositions*. And its semantics is the subset of those combinations which are facts. It may be quite an amount of work to find all *elementary propositions* and to check all logical combinations of them whether they are factually true or not – but the method is a perfect algorithm for the construction of a perfect picture of the world, which is built up by the facts. Once this algorithm is accepted, everything within the scheme becomes self-evident and tautological, and one cannot speak about anything outside the scheme in a scientific or philosophical language. Mystical *somethings* behind the scheme may appear or may be *shown* (e.g. that the world does exist at all) – but the rule is to pass over such *somethings* in silence.

The most extreme followers of Wittgenstein's thoughts went one step further and denied the existence of anything outside the *Tractatus*-like construction: there is no metaphysics whatsoever. In particular the *Wiener Kreis (Vienna Circle)* endeavoured to work out a complete construction of the world in the sense of the *Tractatus* and rejected Wittgenstein's mysticism. The school in general is called *Logical Empiricism* and its centers besides Vienna were Oxford, Chicago, Berlin, Copenhagen, Helsinki and Paris. The theory of languages was studied, including the investigation of metalanguages and the logics of semantics. Wittgenstein's *elementary propositions* were called *protocol sentences* (e.g. "on 15 July 1932 at noon the temperature in Amsterdam was plus 15 degrees centigrade") and a unified language for science was envisaged.

The head of the *Wiener Kreis*, M. Schlick, was murdered by a psychopath in 1936 and the political catastrophy of 1938 removed the circle almost completely from Vienna [21]. Only Kraft and Juhos remained in Vienna and none of the emigrated members returned after the war. But the dissolution of the *Wiener Kreis* intensified the spreading of the ideas in all directions, and today the literature on Wittgenstein and Logical Empiricism is abundant.

Looking on these ideas in the time of the computer, one comes to an important observation: what Wittgenstein tried to construct is the universe realized today in the computer, where everything indeed goes down to a protocol decision between *true* and *false*: to the bit of the computer word. And everything more complex is a true logical combination of such bits. The computer, as a matter of fact, implements the philosophy of Wittgenstein and what the computer says is clear and about what the computer cannot talk it by necessity passes over in silence (but be careful: this is not necessarily true for the people around!). The world where the computer operates is a universe of bits. The Logo of IFIP depicts this situation very clearly:

the stylized storage core – the container of the protocolbit – reflects in the globe.

One could hope – and some people do – that the time of cybernetics and of information processing will bring the crowning of 400 years of rationalistic effort: the execution of Wittgenstein's algorithm yielding a perfect description and understanding of reality by science. But the hope is delusive.

7. The semantic problem

Imperfection versus perfection
or
Wittgenstein II versus Wittgenstein I

Wittgenstein was not only the philosopher who pushed the philosophy of perfection to the extreme. He is also unique for not only realizing that he had been wrong, but also creating a second and new philosophy, so that – speaking with maximum care – the *Tractatus* was written by Wittgenstein I and the new work, published after his death under the headline *Philosophical Investigations* [22], by Wittgenstein II.

Again a little story can show the essential [20]. In 1933, Wittgenstein had newly become interested in philosophy (in between he had built a house for his sister in Vienna – applying his strength in abstract architecture on a concrete example, which God and the Vienna authorities may save from destruction! – and he had worked as a teacher in Lower Austria, trying to check how his views applied in psychology; at that time, the Viennese school system was very advanced). He had accepted to live in Oxford; he did not really lecture, but he liked to have discussion rounds and, even more, to discuss with particular people. One of these was P. Sraffa, a distinguished economist of Neapolitan descent. Wittgenstein one day dwelled again on his idea that language had to be the logical picture of the world and that each sentence had to follow the logical syntax. And Sraffa answered, this time, by means of a typical Neapolitan gesture which not only expresses disgust, but also tells a full story around the rejection at the same time. *What is the logical picture of this gesture?* Sraffa added, *what is its logical syntax?* Instantly Wittgenstein realized that he had been wrong. For the rest of his life, he wrote his philosophy II where the semantics of a word depends of the *language game* within which it is used. The idea of a formal definition of semantics in natural languages and environments had failed.

The failure is not in the logic of the *Tractatus,* it is in some of its more or less hidden assumptions; if all of them had been correct, then the *Tractatus* would in fact have been the end of philosophy.

The first wrong assumption was the existence of atom-like elements in reality, language and philosophy. A simple unit, for which the Neapolitan gesture is one of innumerable examples, turns out to be universe in itself at deeper investigation – like the atom of physics. All protocol sentences have this property. The clear yes-no decision without decomposition is a privilege of the artificial, of the constructed world, of logic and formal definition. There is a gap between the natural and constructed world which no algorithm can bridge.

A simple illustration can make it obvious. The engineer defines his construct by a logical picture, for instance by a drawing, and it is only on paper or in the computer memory that this picture may remain ideal. As soon as it is sent down for realization into the workshop, the real product no longer has the ideal lines, planes, circles and so on, but within certain agreed tolerances it will correspond to the formal definition. If not, the engineer is entitled to return the product to the workshop and to request proper realization.

The biologist is in quite a different position. When he writes a book on dogs, carefully considering all knowledge and systematics of biology concerning dogs, and afterwards he sees a dog which does not correspond to the description in the book, then the dog is right and the biologist is wrong; he must rewrite his book. The human mind, obviously, is even more on the non-engineering side than the dog.

Formal description before construction (only exceptionally unknown technical devices require description after investigation) and informal description of a living structure is not the only difference behind this illustration; others are systems philosophy, the component philosophy, storage and development – the reader will find more.

Another hidden and wrong assumption of the *Tractatus* was that the eternal truths of logic apply to a logical picture of the world. Our knowledge of the world, however, includes a big number of time-dependent truths. Indeed the term *information* includes time: one knows more receiving *information*. Information processing means a continuing change in the picture of the part of our knowledge with which the problem is concerned. But the *Tractatus* has no time-dependent logic, it assumes that a static picture of the world can be produced.

But even within a static structure like an axiomatic system, the perfect order, which the *Tractatus* expected, cannot be reached, as a friend of Wittgenstein and member of the *Wiener Kreis*, the mathematician K. Gödel, proved in 1931 [23]: even in a simple system of axioms covering only entire numbers, there are sentences which cannot be decided.

There is no perfect logical picture of the natural world and the philosophy of perfection is not the solution for understanding man and the universe. Philosophy is open as it always has been.

The biggest problem is the semantic problem. Constellations and patterns, combinations and logical orders can frequently be covered by a formal definition, by an almost perfect description (we can at least find out where the undecidable problems will escape the perfect order). Even the syntax of a natural language is very close to a system of production rules, if this system is elaborated enough (and if exceptions are tolerated). But the meaning of reality and natural languages will always and essentially extend over any formal system. The *Philosophical Investigations* deal with this difficulty. The example of Bar-Hillel in section 3 is not only typical for the mechanical translation of natural languages, it indicates the countless dimensions of the human mind reflected by the undefinable meaning of words. Bar-Hillel once gave me another example for the illustration of the difference between Wittgenstein I and Wittgenstein II; in the philosophy of the *Tractatus* a musical symphony and its score are identical – but the execution of the score is not the execution of an algorithm, the undefined human knowledge of all performing people comes into the play and makes all the difference between one performance and the next. Some of this is in any natural information, even in a scientific statement in informal language.

We have defined semantics as the relationship between the signs and the objects to which they refer. Semantic truth must be verified. The problem is verification; another assumption of Wittgenstein was that verification is possible, in particular for the general statements necessary in the complete picture of reality. Now another Viennese philosopher, related to but not a member of the Vienna Circle, Sir Karl Popper, has shown that general verification is not possible [24].

His principle is that since we cannot verify our assumptions, we are at least obliged to do our best to falsify them, and to accept only those where the attempts of falsification are not successful – temporarily, because they might turn out to be false at a later moment. And more recent philosophical investigations seem to indicate that even this falsification principle has problematic aspects.

There is no algorithm for general verification in the non-constructed situation: the human mind and human education will never be replaced by a computer-organized system of algorithms. Semantics escapes programming and mankind has no hope of reaching perfection. We will never achieve the logical picture of the world for which 400 years of philosophy have hoped and for which the *Tractatus* has tried to give the algorithm. What does this mean for the computer – which realized the ideal of the *Tractatus?*

8. The consequences

Computer, language and society

The computer is a constructed device – both hardware and software – communicating with the real, live world. What we essentially conclude from the philosophical investigation is that there will be matching problems in all future. The present practical difficulties with data acquisition and with data interpretation appear as predicted and explained by semiotic theory and as a part of a more general problem: conservation of meaning in information processing.

Safety and reliability can only be achieved in the constructed realm, in terms of formal definition. The proper function of the automaton does not only depend on reliable hardware: it depends also on the clarity and unambiguousness of programs and data inside and outside the electronic machinery. The stream of information through the total system (Fig. 8) requires formal definition of hardware and software, of programming languages, programs and data. But even this is not sufficient. The introduction of a computer system in a company, an institution or an office under the tacit assumption that the electronic system will perfectly take over the work previously done by people, that the computer is a particularly reliable and indefatigable *colleague Robot* (as a German book title formulated [25]), has a good chance of failing. The computer does not replace man, who is less systematic but much more than a symbol replacement automaton. Man has an incredible learning capacity (which artificial intelligence still does not know how to simulate except in very trivial examples) and, in contrast to the computer, he can watch the meaning of what he is doing and

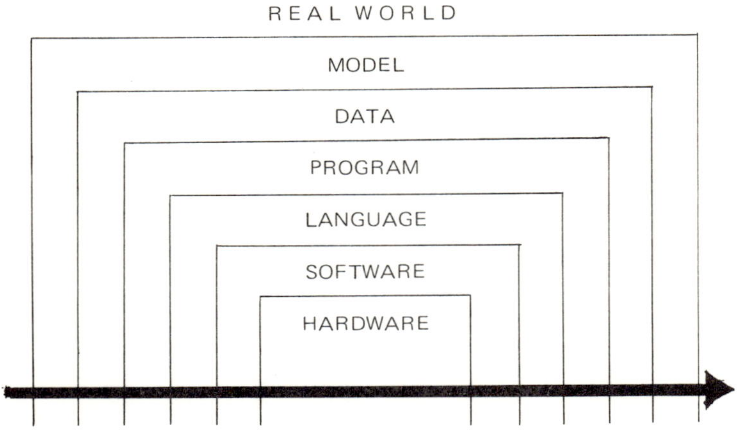

Fig. 8. The flow of information from real world to real world

most of the time indeed he does. The machinery just follows the rules. The problem is to find the most economic combination of constructed and natural information processing structures, in detail as well as along the general lines.

What deserves particular attention is the transition from natural to constructed information, the point where the formal structure communicates with its live environment. This is not necessarily the input and the output of the electronic system. In Fig. 8 we have indicated a level called *model* between *data* and *real world* – the model is not necessarily restricted to the digital machinery, it can be extended into the live world. The human being can act as *computor*, as rational rule-obeying calculator and symbol replacer, as *computerist* in the sense of Leibniz. Proper preparation of data and programs is already now exactly this kind of activity, and we can expect that the importance of such work will increase and become an essential part of information processing.

We will not apply the computer in the future without studying its implications to its environment and how its function will influence the company, the institution or the office. Very probably, a formal model of the information flow will have to be established where the roles of the human beings and of the automatic system can be seen and defined. From the philosophical insight it follows very clearly that the computer does not make the human being unnecessary. On the contrary, no machine depends more on proper, on excellent supervision than the computer. It will always remain man's task to

(1) conceive the formal structures,
(2) get them realized in hardware and software,
(3) get them going,
(4) interconnect them properly to the live world,
(5) supervise and reconsider the achievements.

The gap between natural and constructed entities requires

careful consideration, conservation of meaning in information processing will demand an increasing precision in the use of terms. The languages used in and around the computer will remain a central problem for many years to come. The development of more and more sophisticated programming languages will not resolve the problem; on the contrary, an increasing number of less educated people will want to use information processing utilities and will have to. They cannot learn extreme formal systems. Some people conclude from this that programming in natural language has to be the solution. Our investigation does not support this conclusion. Nobody tries to return from algebra to natural language. It is unnatural to describe constructed relations and digital programs in natural language, it would have disastrous consequences from a certain point of complication on.

Some of these consequences are already here and we suffer from them; we have too much engineering spirit on the one side and too little on the other. We deal with the individual and with society sometimes as if they were constructs, but at the same time we let technology grow into the natural environment without planning and control. A clearer distinction between artificial and constructed realms is necessary.

Information processing could contribute to this distinction because it has so much to do with control and, even more, with languages. And while I do not intend to predict the future of information processing, I want to close this investigation with an idea which came to me when I reflected upon the consequences of the philosophical findings: it could be that the forthcoming society will need three kinds of languages which in some future everybody will learn and master.

The first language is the natural language in which one grows up, it has local character and will be used for talking and poetry, TV and newspapers and many other fields.

The second language is also a natural language, but it serves as an international link, in general subjects as well as in scientific and professional ones – and as far as it is not preferable

TYPE	LANGUAGE	PURPOSE	EXAMPLE
NATURAL	LOCAL	TALK, NEWSPAPER, POETRY, etc.	DUTCH
NATURAL	INTERNATIONAL	PROFESSIONAL COMMUNICATION	ENGLISH
CONSTRUCTED	STANDARD	MODEL DESCRIPTION PROGRAMMING	ISO-FOL

to express the thought in a formal language. The present day example is English, the international language for information processing, aviation and many more fields.

The third language is constructed and rather a language family than a single language. It will serve for description and definition, calculation and operation, including all kind of programming, and covering all fields of logics, mathematics, physics and science, technology and formal administration. There will be a general part, learned by everybody and looking very much like the second natural language, but its terms would have a formal definition decided and registered by the International Standards Organization (ISO) so that the name of the language could be ISO-FOrmal Language, ISOFOL. It would have a special part covering logical and mathematical algebra, maybe continuing the ALGOL and other traditions, and families of professional languages for the different branches of knowledge and technology; the special part and the professional formal language would be learned only by those who study the corresponding subject or learn the corresponding profession.

I could dream up many more details of such a language trilogy – the reader certainly could too. Let me say only that a distinction between formal and informal structures already in the language used for their description and expression might be of help to avoid confusion. Today very frequently the gap between formal and informal universes is overlooked, neglected, ignored. Formal thinking is applied to relations which would require informal understanding and formal structures are very sloppily described in an inadequate and misleading natural language.

Whether the reader accepts this idea or not, – is not important. If the idea once will make sense, it will be in the distant future. But I hope that the reader is hereby invited to pay more attention to what philosophy can contribute to the advance of information processing. Do not share my opinions, but take an interest in them – this is my invitation.

References

[1] G. Boole, *The Mathematical Analysis of Logic – being an essay toward a calculus of deductive reasoning* (London, Cambridge, 1847).
G. Boole, *An Investigation of the Laws of Thought – on which are founded the mathematical theories of logic and probabilities.* (Walton, London, 1854; Dover Publ. S28, New York; 424 pp).

[2] G. Frege, *Begriffsschrift – eine der arithmetischen nachgebildete Formelsprache des reinen Denkens.* (Verlag, Nebert, Halle 1879).
G. Frege, *Begriffsschrift – a formula language, modeled upon of arithmetic, for pure thought.* – In: J. van Heijenoort (ed.), From Frege to Gödel, A Source Book in Mathematical Logic, 1879–1931 (Harvard Univ. Press, Cambridge, Mass., 1967) pp. 1–82.

[3] A. Koestler, *The Sleepwalkers* (Hutchinson, London 1968) 624 pp.
A. Koestler, *Die Nachtwandler – Das Bild des Universums im Wandel der Zeit* (Scherz Verlag, Bern, Stuttgart, Wien 1959) 560 pp.

[4] C.S. Peirce, *Collected Papers*, Vol. 1–6 (Harvard Press, Cambridge, MA. 1931–1935).
C. Morris: *Signs, Language and Behaviour* (G. Braziller, New York, 1955).

[5] S. Gorn: Semiotic Relationships in Ambigously Stratified Language Systems, International Colloquium for Algebraic Linguistics and Automata Theory, Hebrew University of Jerusalem August 24–25, 1964; 46 pp.

[6] J.M. Fourier, *Théorie analytique de la chaleur* (Paris, 1822).

[7] P. Kohout, *August August, August* (Dilia, Praha, 1967; Bucher, Luzern Frankfurt a.M., 1969) 72 pp.

[8] Y. Bar-Hillel, The Present Status of Automatic Translation of Languages, in: F.L. Alt (ed.) *Advances in Computers* Vol. 1 (Academic Press, New York, 1960) pp. 92–163, in particular Appendix III, pp. 158–163.

[9] L. Torres y Quevedo, Sobre un sistema de notaciones y simbolos destinados á facilitar la descripción de las máquinas, *Publicado por la Revista Ingenieria*, Madrid 1907.
H. Zemanek, Eine formale Sprache aus dem Jahre 1907, *Elektronische Rechenanlagen* 10 (1968) No. 1, pp. 5–6.

[10] W.H.P. Leslie (ed.), *Numerical Control Programming Languages* Proceedings of the 1st International IFIP/IFAC PROLAMAT Conference, Rome 1969 (North Holland, Amsterdam, 1970) 461+43 pp.

[11] J.W. Backus, The Syntax and Semantics of the Proposed International Algebraic Language of the Zurich ACM-GAMM Conference, in: *Information Processing* – Proceedings of the International Conference on Information Processing, UNESCO, Paris 15–20 June 1959. (UNESCO, Paris-Oldenbourg, München; Butterworths, London, 1969) pp. 125–132.

[12] P. Naur (ed.), *Revised Report on the Algorithmic Language ALGOL 60* (Regnecentralen, Copenhagen, 1962 and elsewhere).
A. van Wijngaarden (ed.), *Draft Report on the Algorithmic Language ALGOL 68* (Mathematisch Centrum, Amsterdam 1968, and elsewhere).

[13] P. Lucas and K. Walk, On the Formal Description of PL/I, in: L. Bolliet et al., (eds.), *Annual Review in Automatic Programming* Vol. 6, Part 3 (Pergamon Press, New York, 1969) pp. 105–182.

[14] N. Chomski, *Aspects of the Theory of Syntax* (M.I.T. Press, Cambridge, MA, 1965) 251 pp.

[15] G.W. Leibniz, *De scientia universali seu calculo philosophico,* Erdmann's Opera Vol. 1 (1840) pp. 82–85 Gerhardt's Philosophische Schriften Vol. 7 (1890) pp. 198–203.

[16] A. Vartanian. *O. de la Mettrie's "L'homme machine". A Study in the Origins of an Idea,* (Princeton Univ. Press, Princeton NJ 1960) 264 pp.

[17] Baldwin's Dictionary of Philosophy and Psychology (Peter Smith, Gloucester MA 1960) Vol. 1, p. 78.

[18] H. Zemanek, Summation and Future Directions of Associative Information Techniques, in: E.L. Jacks (ed.), *Associative Information Techniques* (American Elsevier, New York 1971) pp. 205–215.

[19] L. Wittgenstein, *Tractatus Logico-Philosophicus* (Routledge & Kegan Paul, London 1922. Engl. Transl. by D.F. Pearson and B.F. McGuiness Routledge & Kegan Paul, London 1961).

[20] N. Malcolm, *Ludwig Wittgenstein – A Memoir* (Oxford Univ. Press, Oxford, 1958) pp. 88.
N. Malcolm, *Ludwig Wittgenstein – Ein Erinnerungsbuch* (Oldenbourg, München).

[21] V. Kraft, *Der Wiener Kreis* (Springer Verlag, Wien, 1950).
V. Kraft, *The Vienna Circle* (Philosophical Library, 1953).

[22] L. Wittgenstein, *Philosophical Investigations* (Basil Blackwell, Oxford 1963) 232 pp.

[23] K. Gödel, Über formal unentscheidbare Sätze der Principia Mathematica und verwandter Systeme, *Monatshefte für Mathematik und Physik* 38 (1931) pp. 173–198.

K. Gödel, On Formally Undecidable Propositions of the Principia Mathematica and Related Systems, in: M. Davis, (ed.) *The Undecidable* (Raven Press, Hewlett, NY 1965) pp. 5–38.
[24] K.R. Popper, *Logik der Forschung* (Springer, Wien 1935) 333 pp.
[25] K. Radwit, *Kollege Roboter* (Ehrenwirth, München 1965) 270 pp.

PAST AND FUTURE OF INFORMATION PROCESSING

by

H. B. G. CASIMIR

Eindhoven

Human civilization can be looked upon as a vast information system. Language, passed on by word of mouth, was for many millennia the main tool for information storage and transmission. But from early times spoken words and messages were supplemented by shapes and images that may have had both magic and mnemotechnic meaning.

As a next step came writing, providing a more complete visual record of language, and finally printing. A consequence of the information explosion provided by printing was an increasing need for systematic catalogueing, mainly on alphabetic lines.

A separate type of information is provided by numbers. Counting, arithmetic, algebra, analysis can be regarded as steps in the development of this type of information processing, many aspects of which were discussed in Professor Bauer's paper.

The information contained in shapes, images and diagrams can be regarded as a third category. Part of it is of course formed by the symbols of written language, part of it can be formalized as geometry and merges with analysis, but that leaves a vast area, the importance of which is witnessed by television and comic strips and also by the simple fact that we can recognize other people.

Seen against this background the arrival of the computer can be compared to the invention of printing with movable type but also to the introduction of the notions of continuous functions and of the methods of infinitesimal analysis. It is one of the outstanding features of computers that they are dealing with two aspects of information handling: with the classification, storage and retrieval of records in written language and also with numbers and mathematical operations. So much about the past.

Until fairly recently one could do almost as well as the Dutch meteorological institute by predicting that tomorrow the weather will be the same as today. I shall apply this method of prediction to computer hardware: I predict that for many years to come there will be no major revolution in computer hardware. I do not think there is a replacement in sight for integrated circuits made by planar silicon technology. Nor do I think that the various types of magnetic memories will disappear, although one can safely predict that for fast working stores magnetic memories will be replaced by semiconducting ones. In peripherals – including large peripheral working stores – one may envisage a greater variety of innovation. Yet I predict that also there such innovations will mainly consist in new applications and combinations of current technology. I do hope that there will come into being computer outputs that have greater aestethic appeal than the sheets of paper coming out of today's line printers which I find rather repulsive.

Let me now turn to fields of application. I shall discuss them from my own point of view, that is, from the point of view of someone who is ignorant about computers and computer programming but who in the course of his work is confronted with the problems and results arising out of their application.

Computers have increased the power of applied mathematics in a most spectacular way. Much research and many engineering developments would be entirely impossible without them. Determination of the structure of complicated molecules and crystals from x-ray diffraction data, designing electron guns and deflection coils for cathode-ray tubes, calculating particle orbits and optimalizing magnetic fields in isochronous cyclotrons, designing thermal engines of the Stirling type, calculating the characteristics of semiconducting devices from first principles and designing integrated circuits embodying such devices are just a few examples from my own laboratories. All such examples have in common that the problems can be formulated analytically, the computer provides the solution. Or to put it in a different way: the discrete operations carried out by a computer are only meaningful when seen against an analytical background. We approximate an integral by a sum, but the notion of a limit and the existence of a limit do not follow from our computer program.

We may compute

$$\int_{-\infty}^{\infty} \frac{dx}{1+x^2} = 4\int_{0}^{1} \frac{du}{1+u^2} = 3.14159$$

but no amount of computation will establish that the value really is π whereas this is almost a tautology when we close the path of integration in the complex plane and consider the pole at $u = i$. In a higher-order computer language one might perhaps formalize the algorithm of complex integration. But my prediction is that for many years such considerations will be of little use for formulating the mathematical description of nature or for finding solutions. We shall have to go on making finite calculations against a back-ground of non-computerized analytical theory.

The most important feature of data storage and retrieval is in my opinion the possibility of multidimensional classification. To give a simple example: from a memory store in a personnel department we might extract a list of all men that

a) have been with the company for at least 3 years,
b) are between 30 and 42 years,
c) are not married or
d) if married will have no children of school-going age for the next three years,
e) speak Spanish

(of course the set of such people may well turn out to be empty).

But from the same set of data we may also prepare a list of people satisfying an entirely different combination of requirements. I wonder whether this possibility of multidimensional characterization is fully exploited. In a catalogue of a library for instance one might add a number of subjective or apparently irrelevant properties like "favourably reviewed by Pauli", "colour of cover is red" etc.

Whereas in the fields of computation and of data retrieval a computer beats a human being by many powers of ten, its performance in the field of pattern recognition compares poorly with that of a reasonably bright kindergarten child. I see no reason to expect rapid progress. Whereas the situation is well known for handwritten texts, a word of warning is not out of place in other fields. A case in point is medical diagnostics. The interpretation of a radiograph or the observation of the fundus of the eye are largely a question of pattern recognition based on extensive special training. There is no reason whatever to suppose that in such fields the computer will soon be able to replace the human observer, let alone to do better than the human observer.

I should like to finish with a few remarks about information pollution. I do not think that it is just a matter of a passing craze or of political propaganda that so much attention is being given to questions of pollution. We all know that all technical progress leads to some undesirable side effects and we are becoming painfully aware of the fact that, when a technology expands beyond certain limits, these side effects may reach inacceptable dimensions and may outweigh the advantages of further expansion. Air traffic leads to noise and air pollution, motor cars to noise, air pollution and stagnation of traffic in our cities. Printing has led to an overproduction of valueless and even disgusting books and journals. I do not think that the danger of overproduction of numerical data and of information is as yet very threatening, but one might as well be careful. In former days our lazyness protected us against doing much work on a mathematical model unless we were sure that it was reasonably sound and gave an adequate description of reality. Today the situation is different and it should be impressed upon a younger generation that they should use the time that the computer is gaining for them, for analyzing physical – or medical, or economical or sociological – principles more thoroughly rather than less thoroughly than before.

The necessity of providing selected data instead of complete data has been emphasized by several speakers. Heaven forbid that I should ever have to read all the trite and dull papers that have been written on one specific subject. But there is another side to the question. I believe that our personality is formed by making a creative choice among the possibilities that are presented by chance. Rummaging in libraries and bookshops, browsing in encyclopedias and dictionaries have been as important for my general education as more systematic studies. Therefore I believe that books are irreplaceable. But one might consider whether we should add some statistical elements to computerized information. In a lecture I gave at Paris a year ago I suggested that a computer interrogated about the properties of hypergeometric functions might also put forward some information on early polyphonic music, on the history of apiculture or on the breeding and training of competition frogs, all of them subjects about which I know very little but which I have good reason to believe interesting. I spoke only partly in jest.

I believe that in coming decades IFIP will have an increasingly important task in dealing with information processing but also in trying to limit the quantity and to improve the quality of the information that is being processed.

IFIP PUBLICATIONS

Graphic Languages

Proceedings of the IFIP Working Conference on Graphic Languages, Vancouver, 1972

Edited by **F. NAKE**, *University of Bremen, West Germany* and **A. ROSENFELD**, *University of Maryland, U.S.A.*
1972 444 pages

Information Processing 71

Proceedings of the IFIP Congress, Ljubljana, 1971

Edited by **C.V. FREIMAN** in association with J.E. GRIFFITH and J.L. ROSENFELD, *Thomas Watson Research Center, IBM Corporation.*
1972 2 volumes xxxi + 1622 pages 110 tables 633 illus. over 2,5000 lit. refs.

IFIP Guide to Concepts and Terms in Data Processing

Edited by **I.H. GOULD**, *Sebright School, St. Albans, U.K.*
1971 xii + 161 pages 4 tables 3 illus.

Algol 68 Implementation

Proceedings of the IFIP Working Conference on ALGOL 68 Implementation, Munich, 1970

Edited by **J.E.L. PECK**, *University of British Columbia, Vancouver, Canada.*
1971 xvi + 375 pages 9 tables 32 illus.

Informal Introduction to Algol 68

A companion volume to the Report on the Algorithmic Language ALGOL 68

By **C.H. LINDSEY**, *University of Manchester, and* **S.G. VAN DER MEULEN**, *Computer Department, University of Utrecht.*
1971 viii + 368 pages

Mechanized Information Storage, Retrieval and Dissemination

Proceedings of the FID/IFIP Joint Conference, Rome, 1967

Edited by **K. SAMUELSON**, *Royal Institute of Technology, Stockholm University, Sweden.*
1968 [1st repr. 1971] xvi + 729 pages 26 tables 224 illus.

Symbol Manipulation Languages and Techniques

Proceedings of the IFIP Working Conference, Pisa, 1966

Edited by **D.G. BOBROW**, *Bolt, Beranek and Newman Inc., Cambridge, Mass.*
1968 [1st repr. 1971] x + 487 pages 31 illus.

Formal Language Description Languages for Computer Programming

Proceedings of the IFIP Working Conference, Vienna, 1964

Edited by **T.B. STEEL, Jr.**, *Systems Development Corporation, Santa Monica, Calif.*
1966 [1st repr. 1971] x + 330 pages 12 illus.

Information Processing of Medical Records

Proceedings of the IFIP-TC4 Working Conference, Lyons, 1970

Edited by **J. ANDERSON**, *King's College Hospital Medical School, London,* and **J.M. FORSYTHE**, *Wessex Regional Hospital Board, Winchester.*
1970 xxv + 419 pages 18 tables 113 illus.

Numerical Control Programming Languages

Proceedings of the First International IFIP/IFAC PROLAMAT Conference, Rome, 1969

Edited by **W.H.P. LESLIE**, *National Engineering Laboratory, Glasgow.*
1970 xvi + 461 pages + 43 page insert 25 tables 168 illus.

Information Processing 68

Proceedings of the IFIP Congress, Edinburgh, 1968

Edited by **A.J.H. MORRELL**, *North-Western Polytechnic, London.*
1969 2 volumes xxxvii + 1650 pages 103 tables 625 illus.

Simulation Programming Languages

Proceedings of the IFIP Working Conference, Oslo, 1967

Edited by **J.N. BUXTON**, *C.E.I.R. Ltd., London.*
1968 viii + 462 pages 2 tables 30 illus.

AMSTERDAM P.O. BOX 1270 **NORTH HOLLAND** PUBLISHING CO. NETHERLANDS

Distributed in the U.S.A. and Canada by AFIPS, Montvale, N.J.